Civil War Nurse

Civil War Nurse

THE DIARY AND LETTERS

OF HANNAH

ROPES

·

EDITED, WITH INTRODUCTION AND

COMMENTARY BY

John R. Brumgardt

THE UNIVERSITY OF TENNESSEE PRESS

KNOXVILLE

Frontispiece: Hannah Ropes, c. 1862. Courtesy, University of
California, Riverside

Library of Congress Cataloguing in Publication Data
Ropes, Hannah Anderson.
    Civil War nurse.
    Bibliography: p.
    Includes index.
    1. United States—History—Civil War,
1861-1865—Medical and sanitary affairs. 2. Ropes, Hannah
Anderson. 3. United States—History—Civil War,
1861-1865—Personal narratives. 4. Nurses—United
States—Biography. 5. Social reformers—United
States—Biography. I. Brumgardt, John R. II. Title.
E621.R663   973.7'092'4   79-28372
ISBN 0-87049-280-2

For Doris Ann

Contents

The cause is not of either North or South— it is the cause of, and the special work of the nineteenth century, to take the race up into broader vantage ground and on to broader freedom.

—Hannah Ropes
December 26, 1862

Foreword

The Civil War diary and letters of Hannah Ropes remained in private possession for nearly a century before being donated to the library of the University of California, Riverside, as part of the Skinner-Ropes Manuscript Collection. The bulk of the letters arrived in 1957 (some came as late as 1978), and the journal was added in 1974. Located in the Special Collections Division, these documents were assorted, catalogued, and made available for research. Curiously, however—perhaps because of their presence at a small southwestern university campus, where Civil War collections relating to the East Coast might seem unlikely—the manuscripts have been for the most part unused by scholars, other than an occasional graduate student seeking information for a seminar paper. I became acquainted with the materials in 1975, when the Special Collections staff recommended the diary as possibly interesting reading.

The long neglected journal and related manuscripts proved to be not only interesting, but also of substantial value with regard to important political and military figures of the war period, the activities of women nurses in the army hospitals, the internal affairs of such establishments, and women's social involvement immediately prior to and during the civil conflict. This complex of information proceeds from the perspective, and focuses upon the career, of Hannah Ropes, an articulate New England reformer and abolitionist, whose name appears to have been preserved until now only in the writings of a young nurse whose efforts she supervised from December 1862 to January 1863: Louisa May Alcott.

Ropes was an activist whose tangible commitment to her principles ranged from direct participation in the Kansas troubles of 1855–1856 to written persuasion and eventual service as a wartime nurse. Personally acquainted with the political leadership of Massachusetts, she was a friend of Congressman and General Nathaniel P. Banks, knew Senator Charles Sumner by his first name, and took special charge of the injured Senator Henry Wilson in early 1862. Had she lived to publish her hospital memoirs, as she clearly intended to do, it seems likely that the unique character of her experience, in addition to her background and direct involvement with some of the nation's then most prominent figures, would have assured her a place alongside Alcott and others as one of the better-known women nurses of the Civil War. She died, however, in January 1863.

Because of her personal acquaintances, freesoil activities, and efforts while on duty in Union Hospital, Georgetown, D.C., Ropes does not speak of the politically powerful as distant figures. Instead, her experiences with them were in most instances firsthand. Her writings present William A. Hammond—the surgeon general hailed as a progressive reformer by the United States Sanitary Commission—as a bureaucrat less concerned for the welfare of hospital patients than protocol. Thomas F. Perley, the medical inspector general whose brief tenure in office won little respect from contemporaries, appears as one dedicated to honest treatment for the sick and wounded. And Edwin M. Stanton, the gruff secretary of war, comes forward as a concerned leader, ready without hesitation to quell any abuse of authority or maltreatment of soldiers by hospital administrators. Charles Sumner assumes the mien of a warm personal friend; Henry Wilson is seen as a generous and responsive individual; and Nathaniel P. Banks appears as a worn but dedicated warrior. Ropes did not know Abraham Lincoln personally. She judges him, however, as an honest man despite his inability to choose effective generals and his reluctance to make emancipation the primary objective of the war.

While Ropes's writings, like the majority of nurses' records now in print, describe hospital routine, personal experiences, and the value of women's contributions, they also go much farther and demonstrate the potential for positive change during that period of women's influence in a male environment. Although perhaps too prone to cliché and Victorian sentimentality, her statements reveal the genuine dedication and spontaneity which prompted her actions, as well as the responses of those with whom she interacted. Ropes may not have been an especially good writer—a statement with which she would probably have taken issue—but the lack of a fine narrative style does not obscure her ability to portray events, persons, and emotions in vividly descriptive terms and to relate her role in taking action at Union Hospital to halt the malfeasance of administrators there rather than merely complaining in private. The matron was a strong, determined person, with little tolerance for any individuals or procedures which worked to the patients' detriment. Accordingly, receiving no assistance from either the surgeon-in-charge of the hospital or the surgeon general in her attempts to remedy wrongs against the patients, she ignored all dictates of bureaucratic propriety and went for assistance directly to the secretary of war. This resulted in official action against the steward and head surgeon, a turnover of the hospital leadership, and better conditions for "her boys" in the wards. Her effectiveness as an agent of change, then, equalled her talents as a nurse. These were praised by Louisa May Alcott in her book, *Hospital Sketches.*[1]

Ropes's materials are further significant in their illustration of one woman's evolution from homemaker to activist during the mid-nineteenth century. Although her statements and activities evidence several contemporary attitudes concerning the maternal, domestic role of womanhood, they also demonstrate in many respects a conscious defiance of con-

1. See Louisa May Alcott, *Hospital Sketches* (Boston: James Redpath, 1863), and *Louisa May Alcott: Her Life, Letters and Journals,* ed. Ednah D. Cheney (Boston: Little, Brown, 1928).

formity and tradition. Underlying her motivation appears a concept of woman's intelligence and dynamic societal potential which was integral to the women's rights movement and fundamental to an eventually greater social involvement for women. Ropes, then, was a reformer, determined to contribute to what she felt was the inevitable elevation of the human race. Social change and the abolition of slavery, she believed, were necessary components of this process. She was, moreover, a feminist, and she believed that the participation of women was required in taking "the race up into broader vantage ground." With goals which were admittedly conservative and within the bounds of contemporary acceptability, she continually stressed women's social importance and the possibilities for feminine action outside the home.

In composing this work I have made some occasional mechanical alterations in the original manuscripts for the reader's convenience, though attempting to intrude on the material as little as possible. To maintain chronological continuity and topical flow, letters and diary entries are arranged in sequence, according to calendar date. Undated items are placed where logic or internal evidence suggest, and probable dates are noted in brackets. Abbreviations, such as "prex.," "Gen.," "Sat.," "Aug.," and "No.," are spelled out, minor misspellings corrected, and appropriate grammatical changes made where necessary for readability. Some sentence constructions were altered for clarification and logic of structure. Ropes wrote hastily, with little concern for form—she expected at some future date to revise and publish these documents—and her writing is therefore at times confusing.

Her commas, for example, are legion, and she often used semicolons to separate a lengthy series of sentences, while at other times no punctuation appears at all. She also habitually identified individuals as "Miss S." or "Dr. C." In such cases I have spelled out the last name. Brackets are used to add words for sentence completion, correct verb tense, insert dates, identify individuals or locations, and indicate words which are illegible in the manuscript. Segments of the original material which pertain to non-relevant matters are omitted, and I have used ellipses to indicate where this occurs. The term "Dr." has been spelled out when applying to doctors in general or to an individual who is not named. *"Sic"* has been entirely avoided.

I have included near the end of the volume a glossary of names—for which identification is possible—mentioned by Ropes in the manuscripts. These are in alphabetical order, not by last name, but according to the manner in which they appear. Thus "Dr. Stipp" precedes "Governor Andrew," and so forth. Most of Ropes's letters are to her daughter, Alice S. Ropes, and son, Edward E. Ropes (to whom she refers as "Ned," or "Neddie"). Other individuals mentioned, other than a very few for whom precise identification is lacking, are introduced by notes the first time their names appear.

Several persons assisted me in the course of my research. Alice P. Van Boven, Ropes's great grandaughter and donor of the Skinner-Ropes Collection, kindly gave me exclusive permission to publish the materials and provided abundant information concerning the family history. Professor E.B. Long, of the University of Wyoming, read the initial manuscript and made valuable suggestions for improvements, as did Mr. Robert Lang, Associate University Librarian at the University of California, Riverside. Dr. Robert Chandler, research historian for Wells, Fargo and Company, recommended several editorial alterations which also helped significantly. Clifford Wurfel and Greg Robbins, the UCR Special Collections staff, deserve special thanks for bringing the Ropes materials to my attention. They rendered continued assistance in making the diary and letters available, obtaining research materials and obscure pieces of information, and offering welcome encouragement. I am also indebted for pertinent materials, microfilm documents, and information to the staff members of the National Archives and Library of Congress; Jan Whitman, Research Historian for the Bangor (Maine) Historical Society; Marjorie C.

Hunt, of the Waltham (Massachusetts) Historical Society; and Elva J. Bogert, of the Massachusetts Historical Society. For the assistance rendered by all of these persons, I am sincerely grateful.

John R. Brumgardt

October 1979
Museum of Western Colorado
Grand Junction, Colorado

Civil War Nurse

O woman!
chafing against the walls of thy home,
and crying out for a larger sphere of action
and enterprise . . .

—Hannah Ropes
Cranston House: A Novel (1859)

Introduction

Approximately two thousand women, North and South, served as volunteer nurses in military hospitals during the American Civil War.[1] Seeking direct involvement in the national struggle rather than the domestic support roles to which social convention and minimum career opportunity had traditionally confined the majority of their sex, they experienced at first hand the grim constants of war—amputated limbs, mutilated bodies, disease and death—and provided invaluable aid to the sick and wounded soldiers and medical authorities on either side. Of those so employed a relative few—such as Louisa May Alcott, Jane Stuart Woolsey, and Katharine Prescott Wormeley—recorded their experiences for posterity.[2] Most, however, unfortunately left little record of their wartime service. They therefore remain in large measure historically anonymous, except for the terse appearance of their names on hospital muster rolls, and consequently the activities and influence of the woman nurse constitute one of the rare aspects of Civil War history that has not been extensively recorded.

That comparatively little secondary material has been writ-

1. Isabel M. Stewart and Anne L. Austin, *A History of Nursing from Ancient to Modern Times: A World View,* 5th ed. (New York: Putnam's, 1962), 132.

2. Alcott, *Hospital Sketches*; Jane Stuart Woolsey, *Hospital Days* (New York: Van Nostrand, 1870); Katharine Prescott Wormeley, *The Other Side of the War with the Army of the Potomac* (Boston: Ticknor, 1889.)

ten concerning women nurses mutes the significance of their contribution to the wartime medical service. Available evidence indicates that their activities often had important ramifications in both an immediate and broader social sense, and that as a group they deserve attention as full participants in the civil conflict rather than as mere helpers of the main actors, more interesting than substantial. In fact, these women often had notable impact upon the men they tended and served under; and, further, the introduction of female personnel into responsible roles in a traditionally male military environment was one significant step in the progress of women toward a fuller involvement in American society.[3] Just how influential a forceful woman could be in hospital affairs is illustrated in the heretofore unpublished diary and letters of one nurse whose activities, unique in detail although brief in duration, were cut short by her death from typhoid pneumonia after little more than six months' service. This was Hannah Ropes, of Bedford, Massachusetts, matron of the Union Hotel Hospital in Georgetown, D.C., from July 1862 to January 1863.[4]

Information concerning Ropes's wartime service has until now been confined principally to brief mention in Louisa May Alcott's *Hospital Sketches* and published letters.[5] Alcott served for a short term in Union Hospital where, according to one biographer, Ropes taught her that bedpans were to be changed whenever used, that the patients' hands and faces must be washed with strong brown soap, and that the men's underclothes should be changed at least once a week.[6]

3. For more concerning this latter theme, see Ann Douglas Wood, "The War Within a War: Women Nurses in the Union Army," *Civil War History* 18, No. 3 (Sept. 1972), 197–212.
4. The Hannah Ropes materials are located in SRC-UCR.
5. Alcott, *Louisa May Alcott*. Biographies of Alcott contain occasional references—based on Alcott's writings—to Ropes. See, for example, Madeleine B. Stern, *Louisa May Alcott* (Norman: Univ. of Oklahoma Press, 1950), and Marjorie Worthington, *Miss Alcott of Concord: A Biography* (Garden City, N.Y.: Doubleday, 1958).
6. Stern, *Louisa May Alcott,* 118–19.

But Alcott learned more than practical application from Ropes. The young New Englander arrived at Union Hospital in December 1862, just prior to the great influx of wounded soldiers from the Battle of Fredericksburg, and witnessed Ropes's effectiveness in assisting these unfortunates. "All was hurry and confusion," she wrote, concerning arrival of the first patients. "The hall was full of these wrecks of humanity, . . . and, in the midst of it all, the matron's motherly face brought more comfort to many a poor soul, than the cordial draughts she administered, or the cheery words that welcomed all, making of the hospital a home." Alcott was impressed by Ropes's genuine concern for her patients, a feeling which was reenforced by the older woman's response to an observation regarding the large amounts of food the men consumed. According to Alcott:

> . . . when I suggested the probability of a famine hereafter, to the matron, that motherly lady cried out: "Bless their hearts, why shouldn't they eat? It's their only amusement; so fill every one, and, if there's not enough ready to-night, I'll lend my share to the Lord by giving it to the boys." And, whipping up her coffee-pot and plate of toast, she gladdened the eyes and stomachs of two or three dissatisfied heroes, by serving them with a liberal hand; . . .[7]

Had Alcott not been of such stature that her nursing activity attracted the attention of contemporaries and historians, Ropes might have been all but forgotten. This would have been regrettable, as her contributions were too notable for such a fate. But even Alcott's statements concerning Ropes are only occasional, portray her merely as a hardworking woman, and provide at best a partial image. Alcott worked with Ropes for just a short period before the matron's death and was not present to record the earlier, more dramatic actions of her hospital career. Accordingly, *Hospital Sketches* and related materials refer primarily to the matron's character as a nurse under routine conditions. Full of admira-

---

7. Alcott, *Hospital Sketches,* 34, 44–45.

tion though these may be, Ropes appears only as a fragmentary figure, without full dimension.

If Alcott had come to Washington a few months earlier, she would have learned far more from Ropes than how to make patients comfortable in a decrepit hospital, for the matron was more than simply a dedicated nurse. Strengthened in self-reliance through the earlier experience of separation from her husband and the responsibility of raising two children alone, she was a seasoned abolitionist, veteran of the conflict over slavery in Kansas, and New England reformer whose political associates included such luminaries as Nathaniel P. Banks and Charles Sumner. The Civil War for her, therefore, was in essence the culmination of a struggle for personal purpose and a reform concept of American values in which she had participated since the mid-1850s. As such, it was a process in which she must by necessity of both conviction and emotional need play a direct and positive part, overcoming any obstacles which bureaucracy or expectations concerning proper female sex-role compliance provided.

By the time Alcott arrived at Union Hospital, Ropes had prompted changes in the establishment through efforts which were remarkable for a woman civilian in a male military organization. Shocked and angered by actions of the steward and head surgeon which seemed detrimental to the well-being of the hospital's inmates—enlisted personnel— she took measures to change matters there. Rebuffed in initial attempts to obtain assistance from the head surgeon and surgeon general, she subsequently ignored all considerations of military procedure and chain-of-command by presenting her grievances directly to Secretary of War Edwin M. Stanton. The result was a change of administrators at Union Hospital, an official inspection of conditions there, and arrest of both the steward and chief surgeon.

That a woman nurse—than whom none ranked lower in the military hospital—could take single-handed initiative, win the support of Stanton, help effect substantive improvements, and prevail despite the traditions of military propriety, was indeed an achievement. For these efforts, as well as her activities as a nurse, she won a reputation for dependability and maternal tenderness among "her boys" in the wards. That she could combine the apparently disparate qualities of committed aggressiveness and gentle concern was no accident. Each in fact complemented the other, and both proceeded logically from incidents and personal factors important in her life prior to the Civil War.

Born Hannah Anderson Chandler on June 13, 1809, in New Gloucester, Maine, Ropes was the daughter of Peleg and Esther Parsons Chandler and the seventh of ten children. Her father was a prominent Maine lawyer; an older brother, Theophilus Parsons Chandler, practiced law in Boston with John A. Andrew and served as assistant United States treasurer for that city; while a younger brother, Peleg Whitman Chandler, was a leader of the Boston bar and a significant figure in Massachusetts state politics. Social and intellectual concerns were doubtless topics of frequent discussion in the Chandler family, and it is possible that exposure to Andrew—an early leader of the freesoil cause—may have stimulated in Ropes her first instance of antislavery sentiment. In any case, through contact with her father, brothers, and their professional colleagues, she must have been well aware of the social questions and reform controversies developing in New England by the 1820s.[8]

Lack of extant evidence obscures details of Ropes's girlhood education, but that she received a good basic training for the time seems clear from her private correspondence and published writings. It is probable that she attended a local elementary school—a relatively common practice for young women in New England by the early nineteenth

8. Record of Live Birth, Hannah Anderson Chandler, Office of the Clerk of New Gloucester, Maine. Most information concerning family details is taken from Mary Chandler Lowell, *Chandler-Parsons: Edmond Chaundeler, Geoffrey Parsons and Allied Families* (Boston: T.R. Marvin & Son, 1911).

century—and acquired further cultivation through access to materials from her father or brothers, as well as general association with her family's personal and professional acquaintances. Women's academies were available in Maine by the early 1800s, but there is no indication that she attended one; nor does any evidence suggest that she studied under a private tutor, although her father's income might have made this possible. Her education, family background, political associations, and intellectual environment, though, were of such a nature that she apparently moved easily among the more sophisticated social elements of New England.[9]

Hannah became the bride of William Henry Ropes at Bangor, Maine, in February 1834. Her husband, born in Orford, New Hampshire, in 1809, was a graduate of Waterville College and an educator by profession. Principal of Foxcroft Academy (1832–1835), near Bangor, at the time of his marriage, he served during the next few years in Massachusetts as principal of Milton Academy (1836–1837) and Waltham High School (1837–1840). Thereafter, he continued teaching in Waltham, in addition to farming small parcels of land, until at least 1847, when available records cease mention of his activities.[10]

Their married life seems to have been intially quite sound. Hannah, for example, wrote her parents over the years that the family was "very happy and contented," that everything was "comfortable and pleasant around us," and that they were blessed with the "true riches" of "a good reputation and very kind friends." And the couple had four children, two of whom—Edward Elson, born in Milton in 1837, and Alice Shephard, born at Waltham in 1841—survived to adulthood.[11]

9. For early women's education, see Willystine Goodsell, ed., *Pioneers of Women's Education in the United States: Emma Willard, Catherine Beecher, Mary Lyon* (1931; rpt. New York: AMS Press, 1970), 8–11, and Thomas Woody, *A History of Women's Education in the United States,* 2 vols. (1929; rpt. New York: Octagon Books, 1966), I, 364–65.

10. HAR to EPC, Nov. 3, 1839, and April 2, 1847, SRC-UCR.

11. HAR to EPC, Jan. 18, 1837; Nov. 3, 1839; April 25, 1847, SCR-UCR.

Five years after marrying William, Hannah joined the Boston Society of the New Jerusalem and became a member of the Swedenborgian faith. With its emphasis upon the confluence of the spirit and material worlds and rejection of Christian denominationalism, this religious belief, which became increasingly strong in New England by the mid-nineteenth century, was held highly questionable by Congregationalist and Presbyterian leaders of the region. Consequently, an air of "being different" attached to its adherents, and Hannah Ropes seemed to find this stimulating. By 1837 she had openly associated herself with the New Church, as it was popularly known, and wrote her parents of the effect this sometimes had. She appears to have looked with anticipation on the prospect of being excommunicated from her former church; stressed the *"power* in the doctrines of the New Church, to *sustain* in the hour of trouble as nothing else ever can"; and wrote how one minister, at the end of a shipboard journey where both were passengers, had shaken hands "with me as though I had not been a woman with a *filthy Faith."*[12] In matters as sensitive as religious conviction, then, Hannah Ropes by the age of twenty-eight demonstrated independent judgment and a willingness to confront tradition where she thought herself on firmer ground.

This tendency to independence was fortunate, for she would soon have need to rely on it. Although the early years of marriage were apparently agreeable, troubles of an unspecified nature developed by the late 1840s and William left his family—apparently, between 1847 and 1855—to go to Florida, where he remained until his death in 1864. His

---

Eliza, born in 1835, died in infancy; William Whitman, born in 1839, died in 1841.

12. Ropes joined the Society on April 7, 1839. See *A Sketch of the History of the Boston Society of the New Jerusalem with A List of its Members* (Boston: John C. Regan, 1873), 85. HAR to Peleg and EPC, Jan. 21 [1837]; Oct. 1, 1843; May 5, 1845; and HAR to EPC, Jan. 19, 1840, SRC-UCR. Ropes's older brother, Theophilus Parsons Chandler, joined the Society in 1839; her younger brother, Peleg Whitman Chandler, joined in 1854; and her daughter, Alice S. Ropes, joined in 1861.

reasons for leaving are unknown; however, health problems may have been a factor. The strain of teaching school and farming at the same time to support his family may have been too great. Hannah recorded in the spring of 1847 that he was "busy every moment" at his labors. He was, in her opinion, doing far too much; and she wrote that "it would be little short of murder for him to continue in such toil another winter." Perhaps relocating in a warmer environment, free from the responsibilities that taxed him so, was William's best solution. Or perhaps Hannah refused to leave New England to accompany him southward. Whatever the cause, his move was permanent and Hannah was left to raise two children alone and fill the unaccustomed role of head of the household. There was no official divorce at the time—perhaps an unthinkable remedy for Hannah, both on social and religious grounds—but the separation was final. That the two maintained contact after William's departure is possible, but available correspondence contains no indication of it.[13]

As national tensions developed in the 1850s over the question of extending slavery into the territories, Hannah Ropes aligned herself with the abolitionist crusaders of New England. This movement provided her life a substantive, meaningful direction it had heretofore lacked. The first four decades of her life had been primarily directed toward family-oriented functions, first as a daughter, next as a wife and mother. Her concerns through the 1830s and 1840s had been chiefly domestic, and her letters from that period mostly contain discussion of such matters as visits to relatives, housework, knitting socks, and mending clothes.[14] The relatively narrow context of family interests, then, had

13. HAR to EPC, April 25, 1847, SRC-UCR. Also, for William's health, see HAR to Peleg and EPC, Aug. 28, 1842. Ropes, with assistance from Massachusetts Gov. John A. Andrew, procured a divorce sometime after 1860 on the grounds of "not having heard from father for the term of one year." EER to ASR, April 18, 1863, SRC-UCR.

14. HAR to Peleg and EPC, Nov. 2, 1838; Aug. 28, 1842; Oct. 1, 1843; May 5, 7, 1845; April 25, 1847, SRC-UCR.

absorbed her energies and formed the sphere of her activities.

Ropes does not seem to have considered this earlier situation confining. Indeed, the role of mother, so fundamental to her motivation and identity, was one which she always cherished. By the early 1850s, however, her propensity for self-direction, always evident but modified by domestic circumstances, generated a noticeable change in Rope's self-concept. Her husband's departure provided her an opportunity for increased responsibility and personal growth beyond the usual boundaries of women's prerogatives; and, where some women might have hastened for reasons of personal security to remarry, Ropes seems to have gained strength from the experience. Now she was head of her family, not insulated within it. This prompted a change in perspective, a reassessment of her abilities and standing within the community, and a consequent determination to extend her qualities and person beyond the family, into the flow of social involvement. Having succeeded in filling the place of both mother and father, she was now more self-reliant, in touch with matters outside the home. She did not deny her earlier maternal role—instead, she sought to expand her activities to a broader plane. In terms of her self-concept, independence, and social identity, then, the period following William's departure appears to have been one of reaffirmation, re-evaluation, search for greater purpose, and a rejection of prior limitations.

The change, however, was gradual. And, had not circumstances provided an appropriate stimulus for its rapid development, it is uncertain whether Ropes would ever have been other than the head of a small household. Prior to the Kansas-Nebraska Act of 1854, she appears to have suffered frustration at an inability or lack of opportunity to reach beyond her domestic commitment and contribute meaningfully to the social reform impulse of which she desired to be a part. Feelings of purpose and a desire to participate were apparently growing within but seemed to lack specific defini-tion, direction, or a vehicle for effective demonstration. "What a coterie I could gather around me of intelligence and high purpose," she wrote her mother in 1853, "if but the power of my own will, were not held in check, by the elements of time and space. . . . why did you give this homely hen, the *wings* of an *eagle?* Behold they flap heavily against her sides, for the want of proper use—and fret away the life which as yet finds no fit element—or finding, cannot, dare not accept."[15]

But if the "fit element" for self-expression appeared nowhere at the moment, it soon came with the opening of the Kansas territory to settlement, and the rivalry between proslavery and antislavery groups which quickly developed there. This area represented the western frontier of the mid-nineteenth century, and the struggle over slavery the culmination of the nation-old question of bondage in a free country. Both created the possibility which Hannah Ropes had so long awaited for a purposeful involvement beyond the family which was at once emotionally challenging and socially relevant. Her son, Edward, journeyed to Kansas in 1855 to claim a homestead and bolster the freesoil presence. This to Ropes apparently seemed the most direct way to participate in the national struggle and also, perhaps, to improve family fortunes. And so, in September 1855 she took her daughter, Alice, and departed the familiar surroundings of Massachusetts for the "Far-Off Land" of Kansas.[16]

It is doubtful that Ropes, upon commencing her journey, had a clear idea of the troubles or dangers she might encounter. At home, sectional tensions must have seemed primarily verbal, intellectual in nature, capable of solution through the process of logic or law. And it is possible that, as with her earlier taste of religious controversy, she expected her daring to be met at most by an opposite point of view. In

15. HAR to EPC, June 3, 1853, SRC-UCR.
16. For a detailed account of her experiences, see Hannah A. Ropes, *Six Months in Kansas: By A Lady* (Boston: John P. Jewett, 1856).

the new territory, however, political differences assumed real and perilous form. Here, antagonisms over slavery combined with competition for land titles to produce a turbulent situation and eventual hostilities between proslavery and antislavery settlers.

To strengthen the freesoil group and secure Kansas for the North, the New England Emigrant Aid Company was established in Massachusetts. This organization assisted more than twelve hundred freestate settlers to emigrate to Kansas, while other groups performed similar functions. Such activity—which also included the shipment of arms and supplies—stimulated resentment among border-state and Southern elements who opposed the extension of freesoil interests. "Border ruffians" and settlers from Missouri entered Kansas to offset antislavery influence, and the result of this competitive activity was an unprecedented sharpening of sectional antagonisms.

It is unclear whether Ropes journeyed west under the sponsorship of a freesoil organization. She did, however, leave home with a party of twenty-five persons, including ten children and five other women. Saying farewell to Boston on September 11, 1855, the emigrants boarded railroad cars and traveled to Albany, New York, where they spent the following night together in one bedless room. Continuing by railway through the southern tip of Ontario and past Detroit, they finally arrived in Alton, Illinois, where they boarded a steamer for St. Louis. Ropes made special note that Alton was "always associated in my mind with the murder of [abolitionist editor Elijah] Lovejoy, twenty years since [1835]."[17] Such comment indicates that, whatever her possible affiliations with any sponsoring emigrant group, she was very much aware of the political implications of her journey to Kansas.

At St. Louis, Ropes secured steamboat passage up the Missouri River to Kansas City. Some of the passengers be-

17. Ibid., 23–24.

came engaged in an argument over the slavery question, and Ropes observed this "snapping of small-arms between the slavery and antislavery commons." In her opinion, "There is not a good spirit shown on either side. The subject is very great, but the combatants are puny; they cannot look over it fairly, because they are not tall enough; or at each other justly, because they are prejudiced." Ropes's self-assumed objectivity was more apparent than real, and her time in Kansas would erase her notion that sound thought alone could settle the sectional issue there.[18]

From Kansas City, Ropes and nine other persons traveled by horsecart—"covered with sail-cloth, not quite high enough to allow us to sit with our heads up"—to Lawrence, Kansas, and arrived on the morning of Friday, September 23, 1855. Here she met Edward, who had preceded her and built a small cabin. He was, she wrote home, well, but—although eighteen years old—"very much in want of his mother." Also, she remarked, there was much sickness among the settlers in Lawrence. Both statements might have been expected from Hannah Ropes, for need of a mother's care and a proper nurse were two things about which she was particularly observant.[19]

Ropes exhibited a noticeably strong sense of motherhood—her participation in and obligations to it—and a characteristic of emphasizing its expression in her own case by nursing sick individuals, stressing her continued dedication to her own mother, and ingraining the same kind of attachment to herself in Edward and Alice.[20] "My mother!" she had written in 1853, "so gentle, so pure, so womanly—I am glad you are still in this world! I could not get on without you. Wherever you may happen to be, it never seems as though you were *far* from me!"[21] These feelings may have pro-

18. Ibid., 27–28.
19. Ibid., 34; HAR to EPC, Sept. 23, 1855, SRC-UCR.
20. See, for example, ASR to EER, Jan. 27, 1863, and EER to ASR, Jan. 29, 1863, SRC-UCR.
21. HAR to EPC, June 3, 1853, SRC-UCR.

ceeded at the time from her separation from William, loneliness, possible uncertainty concerning her new life pattern, and a consequent dependence upon her mother as the one reference point for stability of which she could always be sure. Still, her attachment seems to have been unusually strong. "Mother, how fast I am catching up to you!" she noted, revealingly, in a letter of December 1855—"almost as old now—don't you see? We will live together when we are old, won't we?"[22]

Letters from Kansas flowed eastward to Esther Parsons Chandler, describing Ropes's efforts at caring for the sick in terms which further revealed the intense social significance she attributed to notions of motherhood and the concomitant role of nurse which she had assumed. This attitude foreshadowed the self-concept she would evidence during her service in the Civil War hospital. "I take the place of his mother at once," she said of one male patient. Another, she noted, was grateful for her attention, saying, "I ain't been so happy this thirteen months; 'pears like my mother has come." And two others, in like manner, "both talk to me of their *mothers*. Verily woman is majestic to her children, whatever she may be to any other person."[23]

Reducing her patients in concept to children and accepting responsibility for them in the self-appointed part of surrogate mother, Ropes achieved extended participation in the ideal and practice of motherhood. This, prior to the Kansas experience, was the purpose to which she was committed on a family level. To be a mother, a nurse, to actively serve and control, to be like her own mother—these in combination gave substance to her life. She had cared for others in the past and continued to do so in Kansas. Now, however, this role was expanded beyond her family and achieved greater meaning by being undertaken within the context of a political struggle between tradition and reform. Her maternal qual-

22. Ropes, *Six Months in Kansas,* 122.
23. Ibid., 70, 73, 77, 81–82.

ities found useful expression in support of a social cause of national importance. In Kansas she experienced the reality of the antislavery struggle, felt a sense of personal identity with the freesoil effort, and discovered the means by which she, as a woman, could contribute functionally to it.

Ropes's attitudes concerning the nobility, purity, and maternal qualities of womanhood were typical in many respects of contemporary notions. So, too, were her ideas concerning women's significance for social betterment. Joseph Emerson, for example, wrote regarding the mother in 1822 that "she carries in her heart, and holds in her hand, the destinies of the world."[24] In Ropes's case, however, these ideas seem to have assumed a peculiar personal character which made them at once a vehicle for self-justification and certain identity. At the same time, they enabled her to claim for her actions the virtues of unassailable womanly goodness, intuitive wisdom, simplicity unmarred by guile, and objective concern for her children, fellow man, or country. Not, according to this self-concept, seeking personal goals, she could believe that she acted dispassionately, judged events from an aloof promontory, and formed political opinions without bias or prejudice. On the basis of such reasoning, she experienced the troubled world of Kansas in 1855.[25]

Her time in the new territory was anxious and difficult. And, although she professed to believe that troubles among the settlers arose primarily from disputes over land, her words and actions demonstrated a clear understanding that the slavery issue was the catalyst of conflict. In this process she was deeply involved, and from it evolved an aggressive commitment to the antislavery cause which would culminate in her wartime career as a Union nurse. The argument between freesoil and proslavery forces had previously been, for her, a theoretical matter. In Kansas, however, it involved

24. Joseph Emerson, *Female Education: A Discourse Delivered at the Dedication of the Seminary Hall in Saugus, Jan. 15, 1822* (Boston: Samuel T. Armstrong, and Crocker & Brewster, 1823), 9.
25. See, for example, Ropes, *Six Months in Kansas,* 27–28.

actual violence and physical danger which required immediate, active response, and the issue became altered in her perception from a question of logic to a matter of tangible reality.

Repeatedly noting in letters from Lawrence her constant fear of attack from "Missourians," who had committed various atrocities and reportedly threatened to destroy "this Yankee town," Ropes kept "loaded pistols and a bowie-knife upon my table at night, [and] three Sharp's rifles, loaded, standing in the room." She soon saw the proslavery forces as "mean and cowardly" enemies, to whom killing a man was "not much more than to shoot a buck," and as "cruel, heartless, dishonorable men" who, upon capturing a freestate settler, "would see him die before they would give him a crumb of bread or a drop even of 'cold Water.'" Her hostility quickly grew to the point where she considered it humorous to consider the fate of Missourians who, having captured "a quantity of Sharpe's rifles and four guns" sent from the East to freesoil elements in Lawrence, were unaware that the weapons "will discharge at both ends! How many times, think you," she wrote, "will they fire them?"[26]

Help for Lawrence, she believed, could only come from "the *East;* and, alas! between us and *our* East, there looms up a fearful Ogre, in the shape of the State of Missouri!" That state, she wrote Charles Sumner in November 1855, has "put forth her mean and treacherous hand, with the will to tear up by the roots every settlement where the southern mark is not stamped upon its inhabitants." In this letter—which may have had some influence on the development of Sumner's "Crime Against Kansas" address, delivered in the Senate on May 19–20, 1856—she accused "Eastern people" of failing to lend assistance despite the "patient forbearance and long suffering of Kansas immigrants." An "Eastern person" herself just two months before, Ropes now identified with Western antislavery activists and was aware firsthand

26. Ibid., 111, 117, 126, 127, 135, 189.

that the situation in Kansas required more than political haggling for effective solution.[27]

Finding time to file a land claim, serving as nurse in private homes to a host of patients, enduring heat, dust, and fleas, and suffering briefly from an unspecified malady, Ropes was continually aware that the present state of tension might at any moment become open warfare. This very awareness, however, and the excitement of the circumstance contributed as much to her determination as personal bravery. She sent Alice, who had been ill, back to Massachusetts along with others "who go home to recruit" but resolved herself to remain. Although reporting in December 1855 that all was "dark and fearful," she nevertheless noted proudly that the "determination of 'Seventy-six' " was in the steps of the freesoil soldiers. The "marks of war are everywhere around us," she declared; but despite the fact that "Uncle Sam"— grown "old, gouty, and unfeeling" from "prosperity and too high living"—had ignored all pleas for help, the settlers of Lawrence would continue to defend themselves, "and may Heaven speed the RIGHT!"[28]

The "right," for Ropes, was of course the freesoil cause. This she saw manifested in the future of Lawrence, whose destiny was "almost my own," and both she perceived as part of a situation which "will be among the *peculiar* epochs of American History in years to come." She rightly sensed that she was now part of a highly important historical place and moment. And if she had previously been perplexed regarding how to constructively expend her inner energies, she now had a cause which allowed them full expression. Although she professed not to understand "the ground of our offence" which provoked proslavery hostility—for how could "the right" give offense?—she was nonetheless fully cognizant of the background to the difficulties in which she was now involved. And she had no doubts concerning the

27. Ibid., 150, 208–9.
28. Ibid., 114–16, 124; EER to ASR, May 26, 1857, SRC-UCR.

validity of the freesoil position. Accordingly, when introduced to Kansas' territorial governor, Wilson Shannon, at a meeting in Lawrence to discuss the situation, she replied "somewhat proudly" to his inquiry regarding whence she had come with the statement, "From that proscribed State, Massachusetts."[29] Ropes, then, was no innocent caught up in matters beyond her understanding. On the contrary, she was committed to a movement which had in part helped to create the Kansas controversy, and was satisfied that hers was the cause of justice.

Ropes's well-founded fear of physical violence from proslavery elements was widely shared, and by early 1856 she judged it best to return home until the hostile atmosphere eased. Many women, she wrote, would return with her and not go back to Kansas until things became more settled. Edward, whose land claim was approved in March, decided to remain; but, for safety's sake, Hannah Ropes retraced her steps to Massachusetts. She had another, more personal reason to return, also—"I must see my mother once more— she is of course more to me than to any other person living." And so, departing Lawrence, she traveled east and arrived home in April 1856.[30]

Once more in the civilized surroundings of the Bay State, Ropes kept up with events in Kansas through newspaper accounts and letters from Edward. Antagonisms between freesoil and proslavery settlers moved progressively toward open confrontation. This to Ropes was outrageous and confirmed her feelings of indignation concerning proslavery aggression and Washington's failure to prevent it. In her mind, the federal government had been remiss for not enforcing order in Kansas. She might in past years have absorbed these feelings and remained personally frustrated about not being able to act on them. Now, however, she

29. Ropes, *Six Months in Kansas,* 119, 139, 151.
30. HAR to EPC, Jan. 20, 1856; HAR to Elizabeth Schlatter Chandler, March 13, 1856, SRC-UCR.

knew precisely what to do. The eagle's wings no longer flapped uselessly at her sides. Instead, collecting the letters she had written from Kansas to her mother and others, detailing her personal account of affairs there, she at once began to compile a book which, she apparently hoped, would promote better public understanding of the need for government mediation in the tensions that troubled the new territory.

Ropes worked quickly and, by May 1856, wrote her mother that the work was completed. Despite the fact that her limbs ached from rheumatism, she had worked consistently, stimulated by resentment regarding events in Kansas.[31] Three days following this missive, though, affairs in that turbulent territory worsened, causing subsequent changes to the original manuscript. The outbreak of violence she had so feared occurred on May 22, when proslavery forces attacked and sacked the town of Lawrence. This unwarranted action, which provoked popular indignation among the nation's freesoil elements and aggravated sectional difficulties, prompted additions to Ropes's volume and gave it concise focus. Until this moment, Lawrence had only been in danger of attack—now, that potential had become a grim reality.

The result of her labors was published in Boston in 1856 by John P. Jewett and Company and appeared under the title, *Six Months in Kansas: By a Lady*. Dedicated to her mother, "Whose Life Has Been More Beautiful Than a Poem, Wiser Than a Proverb," and "TO THE MOTHERS" of those in Kansas, the book recounted Ropes's experiences in the frontier region. She laid the blame for confusion there squarely upon "that most *unmitigated calamity* Heaven ever suffered upon the earth—FRANKLIN PIERCE."[32] And, spurning all pretensions to objectivity concerning the slaveholding states and political feeling, she now demonstrated her fully-formed

31. HAR to EPC, May 19, 1856, SRC-UCR.
32. Ropes, *Six Months in Kansas,* 228.

opposition to those challenging the freesoil cause and to the Democratic leadership which, she believed, refused to hinder them. Appearing at a moment when emotions and political differences were heightened by the slavery question, the territorial issue, and the rise of the Republican party, *Six Months in Kansas* was a freesoil tract which Ropes's abolitionist colleagues must have welcomed as a significant contribution for their position in the current national debate.

Seeking to expand her readership, Ropes approached William Cullen Bryant, editor of the *New York Evening Post,* concerning possible publication of her work in his journal. Although he was a staunch abolitionist, Bryant replied in October 1856 that he could not print the material, which he considered "of a merely literary nature." However, he noted:

> I have looked over your book on Kansas and was pleased with it. I liked it for the unpretentious manner in which it is written and for the firmness and courage which evidently formed part of the character of the writer. I should think that you might make some very acceptable contributions to the magazines. If you think of trying your fortune in that way, I will see what can be done with your manuscript at Putnam's, or to do you any other service in my power.[33]

Ropes, though, does not seem to have pursued the matter further, and remained content with the presence of her writing in book form.

Although she still found time to nurse sick friends, Ropes now became increasingly involved in matters of public concern. She took part in political and benevolent programs, regularly inviting such persons as Massachusetts reformer George Sumner and literary personality Edwin Percy Whipple to Bedford for lectures to the public. Her optimism regarding the ultimate triumph of social progress proceeded in part from her Swedenborgian religious convictions. On October 5, 1857, she wrote to Nathaniel P. Banks, out-

33. William Cullen Bryant to HAR, Oct. 8, 1856, SRC-UCR.

spoken foe of slavery expansion in Congress, requesting that he come to speak. Banks responded from Washington on December 11, apologizing for not being able to come at present and noting that the winter would hold "great excitement" at the capital over the Kansas question. "The timid old man who is at the head of the government," he said, referring to President James Buchanan, "has surrendered absolutely to the extreme Southern men and is, if possible to be, worse than Pierce." He was, however, glad to hear from Ropes, hoped soon to see her in Bedford, and concluded by saying that "I know your sympathy and my own are in unison."[34]

The "homely hen," then, who only four years before had defined herself as *"purely domestic,* content to scratch in the *small chips* thrown by, from the abundance of those more ambitious," was by the late 1850s deeply involved in the heated socio-political issues which threatened to split the Union.[35] A published author and activist whose sympathies were directly in line with those of the Republican party, she had—like Abraham Lincoln—found in the issues and arguments consequent upon the Kansas-Nebraska Act a purpose for commitment and reference point for the desire concerning specific direction which had until that time remained unsatisfied. Sure now of what she must do, she became a working part of that movement dedicated to ending the tradition of compromise over slavery expansion which had characterized American politics since the nation's inception. She made the acquaintance of the politically powerful in Massachusetts, including United States senators and congressmen, and this increased her personal interest in current affairs which simple conceptual understanding could not have engendered. If the Kansas-Nebraska Act was the catalytic turning point for the United States at mid-century,

34. George Sumner to HAR, Oct. 19, 1857; E.P. Whipple to HAR, Nov. 2, 1857; Nathaniel P. Banks to HAR, Dec. 11, 1857, SRC-UCR.
35. HAR to EPC, June 3, 1853, SRC-UCR.

so was it the factor which provided Hannah Ropes the cause and direction she had long sought.[36]

While Ropes's local reform labors complemented the freesoil efforts sponsored in the national councils by her political friends, events multiplied to increase national tensions. John Brown's massacre of five proslavery men in Kansas on May 24–25, 1856, compounded the emotional effect generated by Preston Brooks's caning of Charles Sumner that same month in the Senate chamber. The growth of Republican strength; John C. Frémont's quest for the presidency in 1856; the Dred Scott decision (1857); Abraham Lincoln's "House Divided" speech (June 16, 1858); William H. Seward's prediction of "irrepressible conflict" between proslavery and antislavery interests; and John Brown's raid on Harper's Ferry (October 16, 1859)—all contributed to the growth of sectional divergence. Emotions and tensions had by the end of 1859 reached a danger point. Sectional slogans, emotion-rousing stereotypes, and the growing distrust between North and South characterized a national mood in which compromise was no longer likely.

Amid these developments, and in addition to her reformist political activity, Ropes found time to compose another book. Entitled *Cranston House: A Novel,* and published in Boston by Otis Clapp in 1859, it recalled through fictional account many of Ropes's personal and western experiences and reflected the concepts of motherhood noted in her other writings. Peter Cranston Stuart, the story's central figure, is—like Ropes's son—fatherless, yet through patient perseverance overcomes the myriad obstacles before him. Leaving his eastern home he "goes west," to a township of land

36. Ropes's daughter, Alice S. Ropes, was apparently influenced by her mother's reformist involvement. She and a friend, Mary L. Cobb, produced a small, handwritten newspaper entitled "The Cascade," during the spring of 1859. In the "issue" for April was an article on temperance in which the two young writers attacked "that fell destroyer of human happiness, Intemperance."

inherited from his grandfather, establishes a burgeoning community of settlers, and becomes rich. His settlement is threatened by Mormons—"there is not an Indian tribe on this continent so debased as the Mormons"—but he and his followers destroy their stronghold and end the problem. Although Ropes thought the proslavery sack of Lawrence atrocious, she apparently considered it proper to wage war against those she thought in error. Again, as in Lawrence, Peter's settlers, knowing that "their only safety would be in the acknowledged protection of government," request assistance from United States troops; contrary to Ropes's Kansas experience, however, the fictional characters receive it.[37]

While *Cranston House* provided Ropes a vehicle for fantasizing an ideal of western settlement, so did it also serve as a medium for her fundamental concepts regarding motherhood and womanhood. Young Peter, left early in life alone with unloving relatives, awaits the arrival of his mother, Mary Stuart, and tells a sympathetic cousin that he would like to be anywhere so long as it was "with my mother." Several years later, enraged by the actions of some vicious male relatives, he cries out, "Henceforth I will trust no *man,* ask favor of *no man*!" for "All the love and goodness left in the world, has fled to the hearts of the *women.*" Reflection of Ropes's ideas concerning female virtue is further found in a description of Peter's cousin, the angelic Sallie Cranston, whose "woman's instinct jumped at conclusions, over which the wise logic of a strong man would have traced, step after step, with most accurate and tedious details, only to arrive at the same conclusion; though through a more legitimate process of mental reasoning." Man, then, was rational, while woman was intuitive. The first was contrived, learned; the second, natural, spontaneous. Hence Paul Cranston, Peter's uncle, might respond to a loved one's death by offering to pay all funeral

---

37. Hannah A. Ropes, *Cranston House: A Novel* (Boston: Otis Clapp, 1859), 317, 329, 354, 363–64.

costs while his women relatives grieve openly, for "His distress was *masculine*; theirs was *feminine*."[38]

In Ropes's novel, as in her life, woman's sympathetic, maternal nature expresses itself through the purposeful pursuit of nursing. Sallie Cranston, for example, kindly cares for the uncle who had attempted to defraud her of her inheritance; a Catholic Sister of Charity nurses sick individuals in Peter's western settlement; and there also Jennie, a young girl of inestimable virtue, tends the wounded Peter and his friend. "We are all nurses here just now, sir," she responds to an inquiry concerning women's activities. Jennie—like Ropes in Kansas—is continually reminded of her absent mother by the words, "My Mother," on her cup and spoon. Of her—and, by extension, of herself—Ropes makes an example for women readers seeking purpose in their lives. "O woman!" exclaims the narrator, "chafing against the walls of thy home, and crying out for a larger sphere of action and enterprise, behold this little girl of fifteen summers, in whose simple wisdom there stirs but one emotion, instilled by a Christian mother,—the love of the Lord and the love of the neighbor. No[t] only is she star of brightness and beauty to those prostrate men, but the anchor of hope, the 'manna' of their desert, the refreshing fountain, without which they faint and die."[39]

If Sallie and Jennie are symbols of virtue, so too is Mary Stuart, separated from her husband after discovering that his undivorced wife from an earlier marriage is still living. Despite the husband's apparent duplicity, she does not remarry. And—in words which perhaps describe Ropes's reasons for not marrying after William's departure—she tells Sallie, who is considering marriage with one other than her intended, not to "commit the debasing crime of legalized prostitution, for the sake of a home and temporary companionship. Be

38. Ibid., 29, 312, 148, 105.
39. Ibid., 336, 376 (for Ropes parallel, see *Six Months in Kansas*, 81–82), 372–73.

faithful to that principle which lies entirely secure from, and superior to all contingencies; be true to that relation inevitable to yourself and *him.* His you are in reserve, though your eyes never behold him in this life." That Ropes's situation may have aroused the curiosity of her neighbors is suggested through Mary's statement that "there are some ladies to whom domestic disaster is the food they do best thrive on." And if the experiences of Ropes's fictional characters reflect her own, as well as her notions of how right ought to prevail, so does the final statement of the book proceed from her Swedenborgian optimism and give hope for the final triumph of justice in the current "national quarrel" to which she briefly alludes. Time and Truth, readers are assured, will prevail over all troubles in "the furnace of human affliction."[40]

Republican victory in the presidential election of 1860 must have seemed to Ropes a positive step for social progress, for this party represented many of the reform and antislavery principles in which she believed. In 1856 she had hoped as a successor for Franklin Pierce to have "a 'Joseph,' who can hold the reins of government evenly, and unite contending parties by the strong bond of mutual safety."[41] James Buchanan, a Democrat, had failed to do this. Perhaps Abraham Lincoln and the party platform he supported appeared to Ropes to promise the kind of government leadership she had so long awaited. But the time for a "Joseph," who could effect compromise between the sections, was gone, and succeeding months led progressively to civil war.[42]

Fort Sumter was attacked by rebel forces on April 12, 1861, and surrendered the next day; Virginia left the Union on April 17; while two days later Lincoln declared a blockade

40. Ropes, *Cranston House,* 158, 225–26, 387–88.
41. Ropes, *Six Months in Kansas,* 206.
42. Edward Ropes, involved with gold mining at "Gregory Gulch," Colorado in the fall of 1860, was pleased at Lincoln's election. See EER to HAR, Nov. 9, 1860, SRC-UCR.

of the Southern coast and riots erupted in Baltimore. Viewing these occurrences from her home in Bedford, Ropes sensed that the final resolution of national difficulties was in the offing. Accordingly, she wrote to her mother on April 24:

> The stir makes us think, and talk over the time we had in Kansas; when "southern chivalry" camped on both sides of us, backed up by the Federal troops. And our forsaken colony worked night and day, to throw up a defense.
>
> But the South raised her secession flag over our heads; it swung for a brief period, when the boys with Edward took it down, nobody knew when or how. The crime there committed against us, has borne its fruit, in the upheaving of the whole country. And God speed the right![43]

The early months of the war, however, indicated that "southern chivalry" would not be easily subdued, and the Union debacle at First Bull Run (July 21, 1861) discouraged onlookers who had hoped for a decisive Federal victory. Although no extant correspondence reveals Ropes's feelings, her mother's faith in the national cause remained unshaken. "I am not so much disturbed at our defeat as maney are," Esther Parsons Chandler wrote her daughter, in her own peculiar spelling, on July 31, 1861. "Aney Christian Nation that will pitch battle on the Sabath Must expect to be taught a sence of their duty by hard nocks. I hope our people have learned a lesson they will proffit by."[44] Religion, though, had little in fact to do with the lesson of the Bull Run experience. What was wanted by Union leaders was more efficient military organization, and the task of accomplishing this was soon assigned to Major General George B. McClellan.

While Ropes had been active in the socio-political process which elevated Lincoln to the presidency, Edward seemed ready during early 1861 to attempt to take advantage of the situation for his own preferment. He traveled to Washing-

43. HAR to EPC, April 24, 1861, SRC-UCR.
44. EPC to HAR, July 31, 1861, SRC-UCR.

ton, D.C., in March to visit family friend Charles Sumner and other contacts and inquire about the possibility of obtaining the postmastership of Denver, Colorado. Since the spring of 1860 Edward had been mining for gold in that area, had had little luck, and apparently saw an opportunity to elevate his fortunes through political connections. Despite his lack of prior public experience, his mother's friends, together with those of his uncle, Peleg Whitman Chandler, and Sumner's promise of aid, seemed to indicate possible success. But, to his regret, the postmastership was assigned to someone else. Taking the disappointment in stride, he made plans to return to Colorado and travel "thence probably to the head of the Yellowstone."[45]

This proposed project, however, never materialized. Remaining in Denver from August through October 1861, Edward traveled to Leavenworth, Kansas, where he attempted to organize a "company of Rangers" for wartime service. He was not eager to become an officer but feared that eye problems would "prevent my passing examination as a private unless I bribe the surgeon . . . ." His efforts at troop recruitment failed, and he determined to go home and try to join the army. Unexpected difficulties arose, though, when, upon leaving Kansas, he was arrested by Federal forces as a prisoner-of-war on suspicion of complicity with the enemy. Protesting his loyalty, he took the oath of allegiance to the United States in May 1862, received military transportation east, and was mustered into Company D, Second Massachusetts Volunteer Infantry Regiment, on June 25, 1862. Holding the rank of private, he served in this organization through some of the heaviest fighting of the war until released from active duty on June 9, 1865.[46]

45. EER to HAR, April 7, 1861; EER to ASR, March 21, 1861; EER to "Friend Dave," April 16, 1861; Charles Sumner to HAR, Nov. 20, 1860, SRC-UCR. Sumner noted that postmasters were usually appointed by the representatives of particular districts.

46. EER to ASR, Dec. 9, 1861, SRC-UCR; Mass. Adjutant General Office, *Record of the Massachusetts Volunteers, 1861–1865,* 2 vols. (Boston: Wright

While Edward opted to serve his country as a soldier, his mother pondered her possible role in the civil conflict. Having been part of the social ferment from which the war derived, she could hardly remain quietly at home now, writing letters to Edward, sending boxes of goods to the troops, and watching events passively. Opportunity for direct involvement was minimal for women. There was, however, one pursuit which allowed this—an activity for which she was particularly fitted. And that was volunteering to serve as a nurse in the military hospitals.

In 1860 Ropes had received from her nephew, Charles Peleg Chandler, a copy of Florence Nightingale's recently-published *Notes on Nursing: What It Is, and What It Is Not.* "Every woman is [at some times] a nurse," said Nightingale. When in this capacity, she must possess "sanitary knowledge" and be able to create for patients an environment in which they might either avoid disease or recover from it. Professional medical skills were only tools for removing obstacles to patient recovery—in essence, they were mechanical and preparatory. Nature did the actual healing and the nurse was partner in this grander effort, for it was up to her to "put the patient in the best condition for nature to act upon him." Having gained her experience in the military hospitals of Europe, Nightingale emphasized that no one could learn nursing from a book—"it can only be thoroughly learnt in the wards of a hospital." The nurse must be honest, "religious and devoted," and "of delicate and decent feeling." She must recognize each patient's particular needs, strengthen his morale, and make sure that sanitary and well-ventilated surroundings were carefully maintained. It would be wrong, said Nightingale, for one to enter such serious activity for petty personal reasons, from a political desire to demonstrate women's "rights," or out of a feeling that this

---

& Potter, 1868–70), II, 40. For service of the 2d Mass. Regiment, see Frederick H. Dyer, *A Compendium of the War of the Rebellion,* 3 vols. (1908; rpt. New York: n.p., 1959), III, 1248.

was simply "women's work." "Oh, leave these [political, reformist, and traditional] jargons," she admonished her readers in conclusion, "and go your way straight to God's work, in simplicity and singleness of heart."[47]

Nightingale's concept of the nobility of nursing closely parallelled Ropes's feelings on the subject, and the volume's closing words must have given the Kansas veteran special encouragement in 1862. Unable to wield a weapon in the field, she might do the next best thing by taking care of the "boys" who needed looking after, nursing them in the absence of their own mothers, providing the tenderness and understanding which only a woman could give. Besides, it might be possible to tend Edward, should he be wounded, or other soliders from the Bay State. Eager to assist the Federal effort and continue her purposeful activity, then, she cleared up affairs at home and, in June 1862, offered her services to the Union as a military hospital nurse at the nation's capital.

That Ropes could choose to do this was not at the time unique. Prior to the mid-nineteenth century there was no professional training for women nurses, and those serving in Federal hospitals had as their background only practical experience and good intentions.[48] There were, of course, some organizations which stressed nursing as an avocation. The first of these were Catholic sisterhoods. The Sisters of Charity, established in 1809 at Emmittsburg, Maryland, were well known for nursing pursuits, as were the Sisters of Charity of Nazareth, Irish Sisters of Mercy, and French Sisters of the Holy Cross. Protestant sisterhoods were also in operation before 1860. These included the Kaiserwerth Deaconesses, established in Pittsburgh, Chicago, and Milwaukee, and other like groups of the Lutheran, Episcopal, and Methodist

47. Florence Nightingale, *Notes on Nursing: What It Is, and What It Is Not* (New York: Appleton, 1860), 3, 60–61, 126–29, 133–34, 136.

48. See, for example, Adelaide W. Smith, *Reminiscences of an Army Nurse During the Civil War* (New York: Graves, 1911), 125, and George Worthington Adams, *Doctors in Blue: The Medical History of the Union Army in the Civil War* (New York: Schuman, 1952), 178.

faiths. And two philanthropic agencies, the Ladies Benevolent Society of Charleston, South Carolina, and the Philadelphia Lying-In Charity were organized to visit patients in their homes.[49]

In terms of real training, however, very few organizations offered programs. The Nurse Society of Philadelphia, created in 1839 for home nursing and dispensary work, did require its members to attend medical lectures, complete a short course in maternity care, and assist in six cases before receiving "certificates of approbation" and becoming eligible for private duty under the society's general supervision. Still, no organization offered a professional nursing education, and those women who volunteered for duty during the Civil War were therefore amateurs whose best recommendation in many instances was a sincere desire to relieve the suffering of the patients they tended.[50]

The situation of women nurses in military hospitals was sometimes difficult at first, both for the volunteers themselves and the authorities under whom they served. That they were often capable was understood. However, the presence of women in crowded conditions with strange male patients created concerns regarding motivation and propriety, and their civilian status made cooperation with military doctors at times awkward. In order to regulate the situation and provide necessary nursing assistance while controlling the women who might enter this service, the War Department in the spring of 1861 accepted the offer of Dorothea Dix to review and have general supervision of all women nurses.

Dix, from Massachusetts, had long experience in benevolent activity, ranging from prison reform to improving conditions for the insane. Fifty-nine years of age at the outset of the war, she traveled to Washington and proffered her services to the government. Her offer was readily accepted.

49. Stewart and Austin, *A History of Nursing*, 130.
50. Ibid., 118–31.

Orders from then Secretary of War Simon Cameron, Acting Surgeon General R.C. Wood, and Adjutant General Lorenzo Thomas gave her responsibility for assignment of all nurses in the general and regimental hospitals, authorized her to accept for service all women who were "highly accredited, having certificates from two physicians and two clergymen of standing," and directed all aspiring nurses to "put themselves in communication with her before entering upon their duties." Thus Dix—"that masterful woman," according to one contemporary—became the central leader of female nurses for the Union cause during the Civil War.[51]

Dix had specific requirements that a woman must pass to be accepted for nursing duty. Applicants must be over thirty years old, healthy, of good moral character, modest in dress, unattractive, and able to cook. They must also be able to read and write, as helping patients required these skills. Hannah Ropes filled all these demands. Dix's emphasis upon lack of looks sometimes prompted sneering comment. One woman, for example, wrote that her nurses must be "plain almost to repulsion in dress, and devoid of personal attractions."[52] And Dix had ample opportunity to reject many young, attractive candidates, for women volunteered in large numbers and the veteran reformer interviewed each personally. Her conscientiousness was appreciated by many, but she also drew stern criticism. One nurse, indeed, considered her "a self sealing can of horror tied up with red tape." Many doctors accused her of being "arbitrary, opinionated, severe, and capricious,"

51. *The War of the Rebellion: A Compilation of the Official Records of the Union and Confederate Armies,* 70 vols. in 128 books (Washington, D.C.: Government Printing Office, 1880–1901), Ser. III, Vol. I, 107, 139–40, 217, 262, hereafter cited as *Official Records*; Smith, *Reminiscences of an Army Nurse,* 125.

52. Mary A. Livermore, *My Story of the War* (Hartford, Conn.: A.D. Worthington, 1890), 246. Walt Whitman, who served in the wartime hospitals, considered older women the best nurses. See *The Wound Dresser,* ed. Richard M. Bucke (1897; rpt. New York: Bodley, 1949), 42.

and preferred Catholic nuns in order to avoid her entirely. By 1863 the War Department, responding to such feeling, gave hospital surgeons authority to summarily discharge any woman nurse they considered supernumerary, incompetent, or insubordinate. Nevertheless, Dix's contribution to the medical effort was significant, and she earned appropriate recognition if not affection.[53]

And so the women, including Hannah Ropes, came to tend the sick and wounded. Untrained, motivated by a variety of intentions, many brought to their activity the preconceptions that had been so much a part of their domestic lives. Imbued, like Ropes, with notions of woman's maternal calling, mission as homemaker, and responsibility as a bringer of refinement, tenderness, and gentility to a male-dominated society, they in many cases approached the military hospital as an extension of home and the patients as their "boys." Since many soldiers were young men, often away from home for the first time and desirous of motherly care, these attitudes were normally reenforced rather than refuted.[54]

This conception of their position often brought the nurses into conflict with the hospital authorities. It was unthinkable to the majority of these women that professional medical men could exert such benevolent and healing effect upon the sick and wounded as they, with womanly understanding and gentleness, could. This, first, because they were men; and, second, because their work proceeded either from obedience to military duty or a contract for pay—not from real concern for their patients. Ropes, for example, had six years

53. Livermore, *My Story of the War,* 224, 246–47; *Official Records,* Ser. III, Vol. III, 943–44. See also Cornelia Hancock, *South After Gettysburg: Letters of Cornelia Hancock from the Army of the Potomac,* ed. Henrietta S. Jaquette (Philadelphia: n.p., 1937), 33, 122, and Margaret Leech, *Reveille in Washington, 1860–1865* (rpt. New York: Grosset & Dunlap, 1941), 210–11.

54. Soldiers often appreciated the women's efforts. See Wormeley, *The Other Side of the War,* 21, and Hancock, *South After Gettysburg,* 12–13.

earlier recorded her indignation at finding two *"hired nurses"* caring for a sick friend.[55] In their minds, then, the women nurses were in many cases acting from motives purer in quality than those of their male superiors. They were doing "God's work"—the doctors were simply following orders. Consequently, professionalism and traditional concepts came into a direct conflict which found expression in continual tensions between the nurses and military doctors.

That nurses often perceived surgeons as unfeeling toward their patients was not without some foundation. While some physicians demonstrated concern for the comfort of the men, many looked upon them as problems in medical treatment and as objects of scientific interest. Louisa May Alcott, for example, recorded that, although the doctors were not "willfully hard or cruel," one nevertheless "confided to me that he feared his profession blunted his sensibilities, and, perhaps, rendered him indifferent to the sight of pain." Another, she observed, "had a way of twitching off a bandage, and giving a limb a comprehensive sort of clutch, which, though no doubt entirely scientific, was rather startling than soothing, and highly objectionable as a means of preparing nerves for any fresh trial. He also expected the patient to assist in small operations, as he considered them, and to restrain all demonstrations during the process." According to Alcott:

> He had served in the Crimea, and seemed to regard a dilapidated body very much as I should have regarded a damaged garment; and, turning up his cuffs, whipped out a very unpleasant looking housewife, cutting, sawing, patching and piecing, with the enthusiasm of an accomplished surgical seamstress; explaining the process, in scientific terms, to the patient, meantime; which, of course, was immensely cheering and comfortable. There was an uncanny sort of fascination in watching him, as he peered and probed into the mechanism of those wonderful bodies, whose mysteries he understood so well. The more intricate the wound, the better

55. HAR to EPC, Dec. 11, 1856, SRC-UCR.

he liked it. A poor private, with both legs off, and shot through the lungs, possessed more attractions for him than a dozen generals, slightly scratched in some "masterly retreat;" and had anyone appeared in small pieces, requesting to be put together again, he would have considered it a special dispensation.[56]

Objective, scientific regard for the patients could hardly be personal. And this tendency to clinical perspective was reenforced by an order from the surgeon general that all doctors file reports on cases treated as part of a project to compile a medical history of the war. Eventually published as *The Medical and Surgical History of the War of the Rebellion,* this multi-volume compendium described medical problems and treatment in detail, providing valuable information on many kinds of cases about which little or nothing had previously been known. The war, then, provided physicians a rich learning experience in terms of wounds, injuries, and disease. But this prompted an all-too-frequent tendency to view patients as case subjects rather than as suffering fellow men. Women nurses, in contrast, were inclined to react toward the wounded soliders on a more personal level, stressed their need for sympathy, and provided a necessary balance of tenderness and humanitarian sentiment.[57]

Caring for their patients in the wards, women emphasized the importance of familiar domestic virtues, including religious observance, abstinence from alcohol, and mutual concern. Yet, while anxious to alleviate the soldiers' suffering, they often grew comfortable and enthused with the control over men which their role allowed. As one writer has noted, they entered a masculine realm and in a sense subdued their patients. Perceiving the battle-tried soldiers they tended as

56. Alcott, *Hospital Sketches*, 97–98, 42–43.

57. See U.S. Surgeon General Office, *The Medical and Surgical History of the War of the Rebellion, 1861–65,* 2 vols. in 6 pts. (Washington, D.C.: Government Printing Office, 1870–83); HAR, diary entry of Oct. 1–9, 1862; Alcott, *Hospital Sketches,* 34; Whitman, *The Wound Dresser,* 14, 44–45.

"boys," or children—Louisa May Alcott considered them "my big babies"—they often relished the authority and responsibility that accompanied their position.[58] Such feelings were aptly expressed by Nurse Katharine Prescott Wormeley. "We all know in our hearts that it is thorough enjoyment to be here," she wrote, *"it is life,* in short; and we wouldn't be anywhere else for anything in the world."[59]

This exuberant response to their enlarged sphere of influence was understandable from women who, in Ropes's terms, had previously "chafed" impatiently "against the walls" of circumstantial career confinement. But it unfortunately often combined with the various concepts of womanly virtue to make nurses believe that they knew better how to run the hospital than the military administrators. Coming from outside of any bureaucratic system or professional organization, they in many instances saw regulations, standard military procedures, and the dictates of professional medical men as tedious or obstructive, to be ignored if possible rather than obeyed. Why, they apparently reasoned, should such be followed when female intuition—"as unerring as the finger of God," according to Hannah Ropes—concerning proper action often rendered them superfluous?[60]

Accordingly, nurses were usually not hesitant to openly criticize medical officers, characterize their treatment of patients as cold or unfeeling, and view the hospital system as in need of women's guidance. Katharine Prescott Wormeley, for example, complained of having to deal "with every style of arrogant army surgeon"; Jane Stewart Woolsey deprecated doctors whose drunkenness prevented proper care of the patients; and Cornelia Hancock wrote that "I cannot get used to the tyrannical sway of men in authority," noting that

58. Wood, "The War Within a War," 197–212; Alcott, *Louisa May Alcott,* 118.
59. Wormeley, *The Other Side of the War,* 44. See also Hancock, *South After Gettysburg,* 10, 12, 15, 18, 25.
60. HAR, diary, copy of letter to A.M. Clark, addendum to entry of Oct. 11, 1862, SRC-UCR.

she defied regulations to help her patients. "I *will* get the things for the men without orders," she declared, and added with a note of pride that "I am considered the shiftiest woman on the ground."[61]

But if problems between women nurses and medical officers were frequent, the medical service, completely unprepared in 1861 for the magnitude of difficulties which soon appeared, needed whatever assistance the volunteers could provide. Army strength prior to the war had been but about thirteen thousand men; and the buildup following the Fort Sumter crisis, together with the need to care for sick and wounded among the ever-increasing number of Federal soldiers, rendered the peacetime medical establishment totally inadequate in terms of manpower, training, and facilities. Personnel from the "old army" included Surgeon General Thomas Lawson, thirty surgeons, and eighty-four assistant surgeons. Of this number, several went with the Confederacy while three were dismissed from service for disloyalty.[62] And Lawson, who first came to office during the presidency of John Quincy Adams, was over eighty years old. Among the surgeons the average length of service ranged from twenty-three to thirty-two years; some were incapacitated; and around half were unfit for field service. Moreover, peacetime activity had involved for the most part assignment to isolated military posts, and the initial medical contingent therefore had no real experience in hospital duty and administration.[63]

Before 1861 the army had had no general hospitals. Mili-

61. Wormeley, *The Other Side of the War,* 126; Woolsey, *Hospital Days,* 16, 20, 27; Hancock, *South After Gettysburg,* 23, 66. Walt Whitman noted that poor doctors and administrators could be found but were the exception. See *The Wound Dresser,* 18–19, 43.

62. Adams, *Doctors in Blue,* 4; U.S. Surgeon General Office, *Medical and Surgical History,* II, Pt. 3, p. 899. Surgeons held the rank of major. Assistant surgeons held the rank of first lieutenant for five years and subsequently, until promoted to surgeon, that of captain.

63. Charles J. Stillé, *History of the United States Sanitary Commission: Being the General Report of its Work During the War of the Rebellion*

tary hospitals were post hospitals, and these were habitually small in size. The largest, located at Fort Leavenworth, had only forty beds. The need for large establishments after the war commenced, then, produced a crisis for the federal government and medical service. Providing hospitals, trained personnel, and proper administrative proce-dures—which for efficiency required significant time and planning—was demanded immediately in the confusion of a wartime environment. And the question of how to obtain these requirements was resolved initially by necessary ex-pedience.

General hospitals were first established in Washington, D.C., to care for soldiers stationed in the vicinity and those wounded on the battlefields of Virginia. Located in hotels, seminaries, government buildings, and other available struc-tures, these were inadequate for proper patient care but were the best the government could provide on such short notice. By the time of First Bull Run (July 21, 1861), about half a dozen hospitals had been devised in Washington and Georgetown, and these represented the extent of medical accommodations for the thousands of troops in the area.[64]

One of these early establishments—the future scene of Hannah Ropes's service as a wartime nurse—was the Union Hotel Hospital, located on the northeast corner of Bridge and Washington streets, in Georgetown. A former hotel, as the name indicated, it opened on May 25, 1861, when Sergeant Jose M. Navarro, of the Twelfth New York Volun-teer Infantry Regiment, was admitted as the first of several patients. Known alternately as "Georgetown General Hos-pital D.C.," and as the "Union Hospital," it operated until May 1862, when it was temporarily closed. Reopened in July

(Philadelphia: Lippincott, 1866), 116; Fred Albert Shannon, *The Organiza-tion and Administration of the Union Army, 1861–1865,* 2 vols. (1928; rpt. Gloucester, Mass.: Peter Smith, 1965), II, 264–65.

64. Stillé, *United States Sanitary Commission,* 118. For details, see U.S. Surgeon General Office, *Medical and Surgical History,* I, Pt. 3, pp. 896–908.

1862 to accommodate the increasing number of patients, it operated once more until March 1863, when it was finally closed and its charges were transferred to other hospitals in the vicinity. An "unsavory old" three-storied building, with an unfortunate interior juxtaposition of latrines and kitchen which aggravated the already prevalent problems of disease, it was termed the "Hurly Burly House" by Louisa May Alcott and was one of the poorer facilities in the Washington area. Accordingly, its patients were enlisted men—better quarters were reserved for sick and wounded officers.[65]

Conditions in such impoverished medical facilities as the Union Hospital were unsuited to effective patient treatment, and the Sanitary Commission of the United States Army was quick to investigate the Washington establishments and recommend reforms. The situation, said the "Sanitary," after an inspection in July 1861, was grim. Miserable accommodations in existing hospitals were adverse to patient welfare, and circumstances were worsened by the fact that "The attendants, the nurses, and the administrative staff generally, of those at least in the vicinity of Washington, were so unqualified for their positions, that any civil hospital under such management, would have been considered a disgrace to the science and humanity of the country." Admitting the unusual circumstances under which these structures were chosen and outfitted by the government, the commission stressed the desirability of new wooden pavilions and roundly criticized the present hospitals.[66]

65. MR-NA, microfilm copy in possession of author; Alcott, *Hospital Sketches,* 30. See also Leech, *Reveille in Washington,* 222; Adams, *Doctors in Blue,* 169; Marjorie Barstow Greenbie, *Lincoln's Daughters of Mercy* (New York: Putnam's, 1944), 107.

66. Stillé, *United States Sanitary Commission,* 93. See also William Quentin Maxwell, *Lincoln's Fifth Wheel: The Political History of the U.S. Sanitary Commission* (New York: Longmans, Green, 1956); William Y. Thompson, "The U.S. Sanitary Commission," *Civil War History* 2, No. 2 (June 1956), 41–64; U.S. Sanitary Commission, *The Sanitary Commission of the United States Army: A Succinct Narrative of its Work and Purposes* (1864; rpt. New York: Arno Press-New York Times, 1972), 45.

The investigation report, prepared by New Yorkers Cornelius R. Agnew and William H. Van Buren and filed on July 31, 1861, covered the Washington Infirmary, Seminary Hospital, Columbia College Hospital, Alexandria Hospital, and the Union Hotel Hospital. Of the last, the commission had this to say:

> *The Union Hotel Hospital, Georgetown,* was occupied as its name implies, until recently hired for its present use. It is considered capable of accommodating 225 patients, and at present contains 189. It is well situated, but the building is old, out of repair, and cut up into a number of small rooms, with windows too small and few in number to afford good ventilation. Its halls and passages, are narrow, tortuous, and abrupt, and in many instances with carpets still unremoved from their floors, and walls covered with paper. There are no provisions for bathing, the water-closets and sinks are insufficient and defective, and there is no dead-house. The wards are many of them over-crowded and destitute of arrangements for artificial ventilation. The cellars and area are damp and undrained, and much of the wood work is actively decaying.[67]

And conditions had not improved when Hannah Ropes arrived at this establishment a year later.

Louisa May Alcott described the situation at Union Hospital in January 1863 with unflattering phrases:

> Up at six, dress by gaslight, run through my ward and throw up the windows, though the men grumble and shiver; but the air is bad enough to breed a pestilence; and as no notice is taken of our frequent appeals for better ventilation, I must do what I can. Poke up the fire, add blankets, joke, coax, and command; but continue to open doors and windows as if life depended upon it. Mine does, and doubtless many another, for a more perfect pestilence-box than this house I never saw,—cold, damp, dirty, full of vile odors from wounds, kitchens, wash-rooms, and stables. No competent head, male

67. U.S. Sanitary Commission, *Documents of the U.S. Sanitary Commission,* 3 vols. (New York and Cleveland: n.p., 1866–1871), I, Doc. No. 23.

or female, to right matters, and a jumble of good, bad, and indifferent nurses, surgeons and attendants, to complicate the chaos still more.[68]

The nurses' quarters were as primitive as the wards. Alcott's room was "well ventilated, for five panes of glass had suffered compound fractures." Here, "A bare floor supported two narrow iron beds, spread with thin mattresses like plasters, furnished with pillows in the last stages of consumption." And poor accommodations were matched by the staff diet. According to Alcott, it "consisted of beef, evidently put down for the men of '76; pork, just in from the street;" army bread, salty butter, and muddy coffee.[69] Under such conditions Union Hospital was an unlikely place for effective medical treatment, whether one was dispensing or receiving it.

As the war progressed, the number of hospitals in and around Washington increased. Places such as Armory Square Hospital, Carver Hospital, Stanton Hospital, and others housed the disabled soldiers who filled their beds and caused continual shortage of medical service throughout the war. Some, like Mount Pleasant, featured the new pavilions favored by the Sanitary Commission, but those converted from older buildings by necessity remained in use.[70] Nurse Mary Livermore described the Washington hospitals in 1862 as "marvels of order, comfort, and neatness," but most in fact remained poorly ventilated, with too few windows, inadequate patient wards, damp cellars, and poor toilet and bathing facilities; and few had mortuaries, which resulted in the temporary storage of corpses in lower rooms.[71]

To these places came the maimed, sick, and wounded.

68. Alcott, *Louisa May Alcott*, 117.

69. Alcott, *Hospital Sketches*, 66–69.

70. Whitman, *The Wound Dresser*, 16–31; Leech, *Reveille in Washington*, 205; U.S. Sanitary Commission, *Sanitary Commission of the United States Army*, 45.

71. Livermore, *My Story of the War*, 248; Maxwell, *Lincoln's Fifth Wheel*, 51.

Army transportation for these soldiers was primitive, from the battlefield to the hospital, and often complicated or aggravated the troopers' physical maladies. Those who could walk were compelled to do so, while the more seriously wounded were usually transported in wagons or rough ambulances, "that shake what there is left of a fellow to jelly." From the railroad station at Alexandria or the steamboat landing at Aquia Creek they came, "bandaged and limping, ragged and disheveled, blackened with smoke and powder, and drooping with weakness."[72]

The hospitals were especially overcrowded after large battles, such as Fredericksburg, "as the waves of sorrow came streaming back from the fields of slaughter," and every attempt was made to accommodate them. But under such difficult conditions many found it hard to rally. Battle wounds too often received inadequate attention, while illnesses spread easily in the crowded quarters. Accordingly, death from disease grew as the war continued. Typhoid, malarial afflictions, and dysentery were the leading problems. And of the three, typhoid—which would end Alcott's hospital career and conquer Hannah Ropes—was the worst. Accounting for the deaths of 17 percent of patients in 1861, it developed in deadliness until by 1865 its mortality rate was 56 percent. Hospital conditions were not alone responsible for this, but they were certainly part of the problem.[73]

Manning the hospitals and caring for troops in the field required almost immediate expansion of the army medical staff. By the fall of 1862 the number of surgeons, assistant surgeons, medical cadets, and civilian contract surgeons numbered almost four thousand.[74] Presiding over all medical

72. Alcott, *Hospital Sketches,* 37; Noah Brooks, *Washington, D.C., in Lincoln's Time,* ed. Herbert Mitgang (Chicago: Quadrangle, 1971), 16.
73. Brooks, *Washington, D.C., in Lincoln's Time,* 16; U.S. Sanitary Commission, *Sanitary Commission of the United States Army,* 43; Adams, *Doctors in Blue,* 15, 169.
74. U.S. Sanitary Commission, *Sanitary Commission of the United States Army,* 43.

efforts was the surgeon general. Thomas Lawson, who held the rank of colonel, was succeeded after his death on May 15, 1861, by Colonel Clement A. Finley, who served from that date until April 14, 1862, when he was replaced by William A. Hammond—whose path would in a few months cross that of an angry Hannah Ropes.[75]

Hammond, from Annapolis, Maryland, had eleven years of army service when he resigned in 1860 to accept a professorship at the University of Maryland and enter a lucrative private practice. His prior experience, however, was ignored when he reenlisted in 1861, and he was placed at the bottom of the promotion list. Assigned the task of organizing general hospitals at such places as Chambersburg, Baltimore, and Hagerstown, Maryland, he performed so successfully that his efforts attracted the notice of the Sanitary Commission, whose leaders considered him a commendable replacement for the unpopular Colonel Finley. This approval was not sufficient to elevate Hammond above those senior in rank, but his personal friendship with General McClellan added significantly to the commission's enthusiastic regard. As a result Hammond, only thirty-four years of age at the time, was named in the spring of 1862 over higher officers—including Assistant Surgeon General R. C. Wood—to the position of surgeon general. He was in the process promoted to the rank of brigadier general, whereas his predecessors had all held the grade of colonel.[76]

Hammond's promotion created discontent among those above whom he had been elevated; and McClellan's influence in his behalf did little to aid him in the eyes of Secretary of War Edwin M. Stanton, to whom "Little Mac" was anathema. Nor did his endeavors as surgeon general, considered

75. Shannon, *Organization and Administration of the Union Army,* II, 264–65.

76. Stillé, *United States Sanitary Commission,* 128; Adams, *Doctors in Blue,* 31–32; Paul E. Steiner, *Physician-Generals in the Civil War: A Study in Nineteenth Mid-Century American Medicine* (Springfield, Ill.: Charles C. Thomas, 1966), 5.

progressive by medical men and the Sanitary Commission, win him the friendship of the War Department. Hammond challenged the traditional army medical organization, calling for a special hospital and ambulance corps, more regimental and staff surgeons, another assistant surgeon general, more medical inspectors, a graduate school of medicine for army physicians, higher rank and pay for medical officers, and the removal of certain traditionally popular drugs from military use.[77] His activities brought him ever closer to conflict with old-line medical officers and Secretary Stanton; and his shuffling aside of grievances concerning Union Hospital, submitted by Hannah Ropes in late 1862, created further friction with the secretary of war. The climax of his administration came in August 1863, when Stanton appointed Colonel Joseph K. Barnes, a personal friend and regular army officer, acting surgeon general. Hammond was subsequently courtmartialed on charges of conduct prejudicial to military discipline; and, although the accusations were flimsy, he was convicted. Barnes was appointed brigadier general and named to replace him on August 18, 1864.[78]

Under Hammond's leadership, and due to recommendations from the Sanitary Commission, a corps of medical inspectors was established by Congress on April 18, 1862, to investigate conditions in military hospitals. The first medical inspector general under this system was Thomas F. Perley. It was Perley, among others, who would assist Hannah Ropes in improving conditions at the Union Hospital. The inspectors under his command examined medical facilities for cleanliness, efficiency, and staff performance, and made recommendations for any necessary changes.[79]

77. Stillé, *United States Sanitary Commission,* 137; Adams, *Doctors in Blue,* 32–38.

78. Hammond's conviction was reversed in 1878. See Adams, *Doctors in Blue,* 40–41; Shannon, *Organization and Administration of the Union Army,* II, 264–65; Otto Eisenschiml, *The Celebrated Case of Fitz-John Porter: An American Dreyfus Affair* (Indianapolis: Bobbs-Merrill, 1950), 263–64.

79. Stillé, *United States Sanitary Commission,* 125–26; Adams, *Doctors in Blue,* 29–42.

At the general hospital, the senior surgeon held sway. Aided by assistant surgeons and ward physicians, he had overall responsibility for hospital activities. Among the staff were the chaplains, one for each permanent hospital, whose duties ranged from holding religious services to keeping death and burial records. Also present were contract surgeons, civilian physicians of whom 5,500 served during the war. Medical students dressed wounds and performed other routine duties; while stewards, enlisted personnel, were responsible for patients' clothing, ward hygiene, food and cooking, and the hospital pharmacy. Wardmasters—usually convalescent soldiers—assisted the doctors and nurses by caring for patients and cleaning the wards. Contract nurses, usually men, attended the sick and wounded, as did the women nurses. With hundreds of patients to care for, as well as staff, the head surgeon must be a doctor, officer, and administrator. His task was difficult, and the circumstances under which it was performed made it more so.[80]

This, then, was the condition of medical affairs when Hannah Ropes made her decision to leave Massachusetts and come to Washington as a volunteer nurse. The gentle quality of life at home was far removed from that in the national capital. Washington was at the time a military encampment, "a city of barracks and hospitals." More than 100,000 persons lived and were stationed there during the war, and by October 1862 over a quarter million soldiers were encamped on both sides of the Potomac, giving the city a martial character well-fitted to its present purpose. Marching troops, military wagons, and galloping cavalry traversed the city, whose unpaved streets emitted choking clouds of dust in the summer and became quagmires of mud during

---

80. *Official Records,* Ser. III, Vol. II, 67, 222; Adams, *Doctors in Blue,* 158–74; U.S. Surgeon General Office, *Medical and Surgical History,* I, Pt. 3, pp. 955–60. Under normal occupancy conditions, a hospital had 1 ward physician for every 75 patients, 3 or 4 stewards, and 1 wardmaster and 2 nurses for 50 non-acute patients. A hospital of 100 patients had 5 or 6 cooks, with 8 to 10 assistants.

rainy seasons. Contraband slaves from Virginia and Maryland flocked to Washington, which was under military government, as did idlers, reporters, and office-seekers. How different this was from Bedford, Massachusetts, so far away from the realities of war.[81]

Ropes arrived in Washington on Wednesday, June 25, 1862, accompanied by Julia C. Kendall, of Plymouth, Massachusetts. There they were greeted by Hannah E. Stevenson, of Boston, who had served as a hospital nurse for the past year. During the next two days Ropes applied to the surgeon general's office—and, presumably, Dorothea Dix —and Assistant Surgeon General R. C. Wood commenced arrangements which soon resulted in her assignment to the Union Hotel Hospital.[82]

Ropes's arrival coincided with the beginning stages of the Seven Days battles before Richmond. McClellan had moved up the Virginia Peninsula toward the Confederate capital, defended by Robert E. Lee. The battles of Mechanicsville (June 26), Gaines's Mill (June 27), Savage's Station (June 29), Frayser's Farm, or White Oak Swamp (June 30), Malvern Hill (July 1) and other contests from June 25 to July 1 produced thousands of casualties and were, as a whole, one of the most terrible actions of the war. Heralded at first by some as a Union victory, the campaign nevertheless failed to place Federal soldiers in Richmond, and McClellan's difficulties with a displeased administration increased. As politicians and the general wrangled about how next to proceed, wounded soldiers poured into Washington and filled the hospitals there beyond capacity. And now commenced the brief but remarkable nursing career of Hannah Ropes.

81. Brooks, *Washington, D.C., in Lincoln's Time,* 2–6.
82. R.C. Wood to D.C. Page, June 27, 1862, SRC-UCR.

The Diary
and Letters
of
Hannah Ropes

Now is the judgment of this world. Each man and woman is taking his or her measure. As it is taken even so must it stand— it will be recorded. The activities of war quicken into life every evil propensity as well as every good principle.

—Hannah Ropes
December 14, 1862

ॐ   Washington House
                                                June 26, 1862
Dear Alice,[1]

I did not feel like writing yesterday though we arrived here at noon; and on the route here, the country was too delightful a picture for me to take other notes than in my memory.

Besides, the cars rocked so, one could not *drink* even, without taking more on to the lap than in the mouth.

Miss Stevenson gave us a most cordial welcome, and rooms at this house till we are rested and our work is arranged.[2]

Preparation is made for eight thousand sick and wounded soldiers, beside the five thousand now here. Rumors are rife that the ball has opened at Richmond, and there is much anxious inquiry without satisfactory answer.[3]

Strange to say, the first work offered me was to nurse General Wilson, who, a few hours before my arrival, fell in a fainting fit in the entry.[4] Tell Aunt Eliza I used the whole of her bottle of annice over his head and arm, for he was a good deal hurt by the fall and is unable to rise this morning.[5]

Yesterday after dinner I went into the Senate chamber and

1. This was Alice Ropes, her daughter.
2. Ropes arrived with Julia C. Kendall, of Plymouth, Mass. Hannah E. Stevenson, a volunteer nurse from Boston, 46 years old in 1861, became Ropes's roommate at Union Hospital. To her, Louisa May Alcott dedicated *Hospital Sketches*. See Federal Census for 1860, Boston, Ward 6, J. Thomas Stevenson household, M653–521, FRC.
3. For numbers of patients in areas including Washington and Alexandria in Aug. 1862, see *Official Records,* Ser. III, Vol. II, 389. Ropes refers to the Battle of Mechanicsville, east of Richmond. See E.B. Long with Barbara Long, *The Civil War Day by Day: An Almanac, 1861–1865* (Garden City, N.Y.: Doubleday, 1971), 230–31.
4. Henry Wilson, senator from Massachusetts and chairman of the Senate Committee on Military Affairs during the Civil War, was a brigadier general in the state militia.
5. Ropes refers to her sister-in-law, Elizabeth Schlatter Chandler, wife of Theophilus Parsons Chandler. When writing to her mother, Ropes used the term, "sister Eliza." See Ropes, *Six Months in Kansas,* 10.

49

heard an animated discussion between Dixon, of
Connecticut, Wade, of Ohio, and Hale, of New Hampshire.
The first argues well in remarkably good language; the
second is strong but rough and noisy, with a voice like forty
coffee mills. The third owes his success to a good cause, an
honest purpose, a cheerful spirit and a fine presence.[6]

Sumner rushed into the vestibule to shake hands with me,
. . . and spent a half hour with me. While waiting to receive
my summons today I shall sit in the House and study some
more faces. Washington is decidedly the ugliest and dirtiest
city I ever saw. One finds nothing pleasant until you mount
the Capitol and look off over the open beautiful country. The
grounds at the base of the building are quite well laid out
with shade trees, and just passibly kept. . . .[7]

[Probably July 3, 1862]

Dear Alice,
It is almost dark, but I will begin a note to you, though I
have heard nothing from you. Washington was never so sad
as today! The news from Richmond is so fearfully bloody.
One of McClellan's staff has just arrived to see the President.

It is astonishing to see the *Boston Journal* jubilant over a
"victory" which leaves twenty thousand of our men on the
field, dead or wounded.[8] I have been to the hospitals and
seen some of the "first" who told me that our friends were

6. These were Senators James Dixon, of Connecticut; Benjamin F.
Wade, of Ohio; and John P. Hale, of New Hampshire. Prompted by the
confiscation bills before Congress, they debated the relative powers of
Congress and the President.

7. Charles Sumner, United States senator from Massachusetts, was
chairman of the Senate Foreign Relations Committee during the Civil War.
Noah Brooks, a newspaper correspondent writing in March 1863, called
Washington "probably the dirtiest and most ill-kept borough in the United
States." See *Washington, D.C., in Lincoln's Time*, 294.

8. The *Boston Journal* reported the "Complete Success of Our Army" on
July 1, 1862. Union losses for the Seven Days were about 16,000 including
1,734 killed, 8,062 wounded, and 6,053 missing. Long and Long, *The Civil
War Day by Day*, 235.

unhurt up to Thursday [June 26]. But the fight has been so severe since that we must prepare for the worst.[9]

I have made many friends here who will keep me informed as far as possible.

Wilson is now out of danger, and I shall sleep at the hospital tonight but pass the days with him till he is in his place at the Senate.

I am very glad of this opportunity to know him. He said, when very sick, that I was sent here to take care of him and I believe him. Officers and Senators are at the door in squads every day to see him, Sumner twice a day—and I wish those who think he has no heart could see his fond tenderness of this sick man.

Mr. Hooper brought some nice wine, which I now give him freely.[10] It is the first he ever drank and the effect is truly wonderful. Chase came and had a whispered talk with him yesterday. He is old looking, not handsome, but very sensible looking. . . . I go out to my meals with Buffington, the member from Fall River. He is a very handsome, large man, and as good as gold. He it was who took up Sumner in the Senate chamber when he was struck and carried him to his home, washed his bleeding head, and stripped off his bloody clothes, which he tells me were wet with his blood. . . .[11]

[Letter Continued]
July 6, 1862

9. The 1st Mass. Volunteer Infantry Regiment, to which Ropes apparently refers, saw action near Richmond, Va., at Seven Pines (May 31–June 1), Oak Grove (June 25), Savage's Station (June 29), White Oak Swamp and Glendale (June 30), and Malvern Hill (July 1). Dyer, *Compendium*, III, 1248.

10. This was most likely Samuel Hooper, Republican congressman from Massachusetts.

11. Ropes refers to Salmon P. Chase, secretary of the Treasury, and James Buffington, congressman from Massachusetts, and to Preston Brooks's notorious caning of Charles Sumner on May 22, 1856, following his "Crime Against Kansas" speech.

I came here on the morning of the [fourth].[12] Found this great castle of a hotel in charge of a very handsome, tall, dark eyed young surgeon from Maryland. He was gracious, took me over the establishment, and talked very pleasantly. He thought I should be better off to go back to Washington House, but I told him I had come to spend the "fourth" here and it did not depend upon "dinner" at all.[13] The nurses had all gone out on a ramble, so I went to my room, and at 12 the sergeant sent me a tray with "rations" consisting of a slice of boiled beef, served on a tin plate, and a white pint bowl of *tea* without milk, and a loaf of excellent bread.

I ate a few bites of it, and then laid down [and] fell asleep. A tap at the door brought me up quickly. It was the sergeant, come to say the wounded were on their way, and we must get ready. Some of the nurses were away, and the way I took shirts, drawers, and stockings out of the boxes, the young doctor, tearing off the covers, was up to the top of my speed. Nurses drifted in and caught the piles of unwashed cotton and we laid out a piece of each upon every bed till the end of our supply, then sent to the church across the street for enough to make up 150 pieces. Only six patients arrived that night, and we went to bed expecting to be called every moment.[14] Of course I watched. But the morning came and no men. We in an hour felt as though they never would come. I went into Washington on business. Miss Stevenson went out to buy some soap, dishes, a water pail and foot tub for our room. I hurried back, and just as she and I had begun to "fix up" our room there came a quick step over our private stairs

12. The manuscript reads that she arrived on the "fifth," but internal evidence indicates that it was July 4, 1862.

13. The doctor to whom Ropes refers was John S. Billings, assistant surgeon, U.S. Army, who served at Union Hospital from Feb. 15 to March 27, 1862 and was in charge of the establishment from May 9 to July 16, 1862. Also present at this time were Acting Assistant Surgeons William W. Hays and Charles W. Carrier, and Medical Cadets Edward Curtis and Edward Storror. IMO-NA.

14. Six patients—five privates and a sergeant—were admitted to Union Hospital on July 4, 1862. MR-NA.

in a wing of the "castle," and a voice—"all of the nurses report at the office of the surgeon." When we ran down the main hall stairs, such a sight met our eyes as I hope you will never witness. From the broad open entrance into the hall, to the base of the staircase, there bent, clung, and stood, in dumb silence, fifty soldiers, grim, dirty, muddy, and wounded.[15]

I thought of Neddie, when he came down from the mountains, and it seemed as though these were he, in fifty duplicates.[16]

Miss Stevenson ran to the kitchen for the warm tea. I stood by the doctor as he took the name of each and handed each his bed with a ticket. Then they were led or lifted up over the great staircase, winding along, some to the ballroom, others to the banqueting room.[17] When all were up, we each took our portion and commenced to wash them. We were four hours. Everything they had on was stripped off—and, weak, helpless as babes, they sank upon us to care for them. With broken arms and wounded feet, thighs, and fingers, it was no easy job to do gently. One quite old man, sick every way, and a bullet hole through his right hand, called me "good mother" when I laid his head on his pillow, and soon he slept as though he had come to the end of war, unto a haven of rest.[18] That was the experience of one day—5th of July, 1862. You will live to tell your children of this.

Today, the Sabbath, I sit in the great hall writing to you, with interruptions all the time. Whatever is wanted I am asked for, and twice I have been the rounds to see how everyone is. Miss Stevenson is a true disciple of Him who

15. Forty-seven patients, from New York, New Hampshire, Michigan, Pennsylvania, and Rhode Island, suffering from wounds, "debilitas," and rheumatism, arrived at Union Hospital on July 5, 1862. MR-NA.

16. Ropes refers to her son, Edward E. Ropes, as "Ned," or "Neddie," throughout the manuscripts.

17. All patients were registered before being hospitalized. See Alcott, *Hospital Sketches,* 34

18. The vision of the nurse as a mother surrogate was frequent among patients and emphasized by the nurses. See Livermore, *My Story of the War,* 243, and Wood, "The War Within a War," 201–3.

thought it not beneath Him to gird with a towel and wash His disciples' feet. Miss Kendall, her friend, is lovely, endowed with the same spirit.[19] The other nurses are common women who reckon their pay and have eyes open to see if we fare better than they.

We are expecting a hundred more today. All we now have were in Porter's division and are from Michigan and Pennsylvania.[20] When one of the Michigan boys with a *dreadful* arm was led in to give his name, I lifted the canteen from his neck and he said, "Oh lady! there are three other boys from the same place with me, *do* let them lie down close by me." And he was not willing to move any till they came, so I went among them all and asked for the "boys who came from Michigan" and all the four had broken arms! I took hold of their sleeveless coats and led them all up together. Every time I go by them they smile upon me their thanks, for their cots are side by side.

. . . Write me, "Care of Hon. James Buffington, Member of Congress," and you need not pay postage. Love to all,

Your loving mother.

> Sabbath
> July 13, 1862
> Union Hospital, Georgetown

Dear Alice,

I intended to write ever so much today but this day is like all others here, except that we look particularly clean. The wards are all washed and the halls, too, on Saturday, and this morning, thanks for the goods from Boston, everybody has

19. This was Julia C. Kendall, a volunteer nurse from Plymouth, Mass. MR-NA.

20. Brig. Gen. Fitz-John Porter commanded a division of the III Corps in the Army of the Potomac during the Peninsula campaign, and the V Corps during the Seven Days. See Ezra J. Warner, *Generals in Blue: Lives of the Union Commanders* (Baton Rouge: Louisiana State Univ. Press, 1964), 379.

on a clean suit. I hold the key of [the storeroom containing] the wines and the clothing, bedding, &c,[21] and go to every patient several times each day; feed those who can bear them, with wine or brandy punch, as the surgeons direct; and dole with my own hand a good many quarts of fruit, sent in by the ladies for the soldiers.[22] I do this because it is a pleasure to me, also because there is almost universal complaint that delicacies sent to the patients are eaten by the nurses and surgeons. It shall not be so here.[23] I had just finished my round of giving out clean handkerchiefs when I halted by the bed of a little drummer boy from Augusta, Maine, in order that he might choose a handkerchief to please his fancy (for you must know Mr. Barnard sent us three hundred) when the man in the next bed said he had asked for me several times, for he noted my face the day he crept into the front hall.[24] The fact is, the washing and putting of a man into a clean white shirt and drawers, and stretching him on a thoroughly white bed, so completely transforms him that I find it hard to tell which is which. So I sat down by the side of

21. From the storeroom men drew tobacco, games, stationery, and other items with which to pass time. See Woolsey, *Hospital Days,* 36.

22. Gifts of clothing and food were highly useful in the hospitals. Stimulants, such as brandy, wine, spices, and lemon, and a punch made of condensed milk and whiskey were valuable aids. According to Katharine Prescott Wormeley, the nurse should be remembered in poetry by this example:

> A lady with a *flask* shall stand,
> Beef-tea and punch in either hand,—
> Heroic mass of Mud
> And dirt and stains and blood!

See Wormeley, *The Other Side of the War,* 164, and 20, 27, 69, 118, 123, 185; Woolsey, *Hospital Days,* 55; EPC to HAR, Oct. 29, 1862, and Mary L. Blair [?] to HAR, July 12, 1862, SRC-UCR.

23. Abuse of enlisted patients and theft of their goods by hospital attendants was a common complaint. See Whitman, *The Wound Dresser,* 159. Ropes tried to protect the men from this problem, having their valuables sealed in envelopes and placed in her care until the soldiers left the hospital. See Alcott, *Hospital Sketches,* 44.

24. The gentleman to whom Ropes refers was either James M. Barnard

this man and learned that he was from Worcester, was one of the "fifteenth" and knew Derby very well, and loves him very much: speaks in the warmest praise of him. He says Derby has been in the hospital at Harrison's Landing for a month, but has an excellent servant to take care of him and will soon be out again.[25] Then the little drummer boy told me about {Jamie?} Lowell, and his bravery, and his death.[26] He said, "It beat all, how the Massachusetts boys did put in." Only, said he, the rebels won't release one of them, for they say they are all sharp shooters. None of our men feel defeated at all by the battles near Richmond, and those who are not disabled for life wish to go back as soon as they are well enough.

My store room opens into the great hall. As I turned the key two hours since, in order to go with my servant up to "17" and take some milk with dry toast, I turned to face not only the toast and milk, but Messers. Rice, Alley, {and} Train, of the Massachusetts delegation in Congress![27] I had seen them often in Wilson's room and was glad to have them call to see me. I had presented the case of extra clothes for returned wounded soldiers before, and now showed them

(see Barnard to HAR, Oct. 2, 1862, SRC-UCR) or Boston merchant George M. Barnard (see note 37).

25. Capt. Richard Derby joined the 15th Mass. Volunteer Infantry Regiment on Aug. 1, 1861. The regiment saw service, during the Seven Days Battles near Richmond, at Peach Orchard (near Fair Oaks) and Savage's Station (June 29), White Oak Swamp and Glendale (June 30), and Malvern Hill (July 1), and was at Harrison's Landing, on the James River about 18 miles southeast of Richmond, until Aug. 15, 1862. See Mass. Adjutant General Office, *Record of the Massachusetts Volunteers,* II, 202–3, and Dyer, *Compendium,* III, 1253.

26. Apparently 1st Lieut. James J. Lowell, of the 20th Mass. Volunteer Infantry Regiment, who died on July 6, 1862, of wounds suffered at Malvern Hill on July 1. See Mass. Adjutant General Office, *Record of the Massachusetts Volunteers,* II, 333, and U.S. Adjutant General Office, *Official Army Register of the Volunteer Force of the United States Army for the Years 1861, '62, '63, '64, '65,* 8 vols. (Washington, D.C.: Adjutant General Office, 1865–67), I, 177–78.

27. Ropes refers to Congressmen Alexander H. Rice, John B. Alley, and Charles R. Train, of Massachusetts.

our men in the rear court, able to walk about but minus coats, and pants, and shoes. They told me the bill has passed both houses.

Wilson rode out a few days since—his gratitude is perfectly overwhelming—and some of his friends asked me what I did to him to change him so! When I left him for a few hours at night he did not rest, but frightened his watchers by his willful impetuosity. At four, I would go in, find the bed all in a heap, smoothe it nicely, turn the watcher out, take his hands in mine, and he would fall gently to sleep and remain so till eight. Buffington said he should like to know what the power was. I said I did not know, unless it was that all the men who came in were frightened to their wits ends about the country and acted as though they thought God was dead, whereas I had the constant assurance that there was a good Pilot at the Helm. In reply he said, several times, "I must have you tell me about this New Church business." But Wilson would lie as glum as a great polar bear, and as dark as a thunder cloud; and when you "reckoned" it time for a "clap" you would be startled and thrilled with the sudden lifting of the lids over eyes moist with tears, and the parting of the trembling lips with the sweet smile often seen on the face of the dying, and without a word he would put out his hand and reach for mine, and then like a quieted child sleep again.

I stopped here to listen to one of the night nurses; she says, "I want to speak to you about the man with a bad foot in the dining room. He could not go to sleep last night and was dreadful fussy." "Well," I said, "you should have sat down by him and held his hand awhile—it is not easy to go to sleep with so many in the room." "Law! is that the way? He kept a asking for the woman with the cap on, and said she could always do something for a fellow."[28]

The healing process is very slow. When they first come they appear to gain because we feed them and tend so well

28. Ropes was apparently popular with the patients. See Alcott, *Hospital Sketches,* 34.

their wounds, but soon the suppuration takes place, lead has to be probed for, and then they get sad and lose their appetite. Our men are all fine specimens. Miss Stevenson, who has been in the army a year, says the heroes are in the ranks.

I am very anxious about Charlie.[29] Wilson sent his clerk to hunt for information in the hospitals of Washington, and learned from one of the privates that he was wounded in the shoulder and taken prisoner and, he thinks, is in Richmond. If Thoph or Peleg can find out about it I shall leave everything and go on.[30] I have learned now how to take care of a shoulder wound. They are slow to cure and must have many dressings a day. Indeed, I had no idea it was such a slow and painful process—the uncertainty about what is in the wound, the waiting for the indications suppuration alone furnishes. We have one man with a shoulder wound who has just been put under the influence of ether and not only a bullet was dug out under his shoulder blade but a piece of his coat. Since that he has discharged at least a pint a day. We put *three* clean dressings and a shirt upon him daily, cutting the shirt open on the shoulder, down in front, and taking out the left sleeve. All of these shirts and bandages have to be thrown away, they are so offensive. Let me know if possible where Charlie is, and if I can go to him.

[Letter Continued]
July 16, 1862

I have been sick since the Sabbath with bowel complaint, and in bed. But am up today all right. Everybody was over

29. Maj. Charles Peleg Chandler, of the 1st Mass. Volunteer Infantry Regiment, was Ropes's nephew. He was killed at Glendale, Va., on June 30, 1862. See Mass. Adjutant General Office, *Record of the Massachusetts Volunteers,* II, 2.

30. "Thoph" and "Peleg" were Ropes's brothers, Theophilus Parsons Chandler and Peleg Whitman Chandler. Members of the family, having incomplete information, believed Charles Peleg Chandler to be still alive. See ASR to EER, Aug. 2, 1862, and EPC to HAR, Nov. 19, 1862, SRC-UCR.

anxious and kind to me. I could not help comparing the unselfish consideration of these weary nurses with my sicknesses at 52 last winter.[31] But that has passed like a painful dream. Do not feel in the least anxious about me. Mr. Barrett, of Worcester, leaves today. He is of the 15th. . . . He is a very fine man.[32]

. . . Write often as you can and tell Fannie to write the boys to bring Charlie here if they find him, as I have power here to do everything for him.[33]

Your Mother

• Although Hannah Ropes was clearly dedicated to serving her patients, she also hoped for the opportunity to care for any friends or relatives who might require hospitalization. Through her contacts with such persons as Charles Sumner and Henry Wilson it is possible that she may have been able to have particular individuals assigned to Union Hospital. From her home in Boston, Alice Ropes seemed to feel that a wounded soldier might designate the hospital to which he wished to be taken. Her brother, Edward, was in the vicinity of Washington, D.C., during early August 1862, and she accordingly wrote to him that "If you should be sick or wounded, make them carry you to mother's hospital, 'The Union,' in Georgetown. I wrote you all about her going," she continued, "but suppose you have not received the letter. She likes the work very much and is doing a great deal of good."[34] Such considerations,

31. According to Alcott, nurses did "the hardest work of any part of the army, except the mules." *Hospital Sketches,* 100.

32. Pvt. Richard Barrett, of the 15th Mass. Volunteer Infantry Regiment, was released from the army because of disability on July 11, 1862. See Mass. Adjutant General Office, *Record of the Massachusetts Volunteers,* I, 218.

33. Ropes refers to her niece, Frances Vaughan Chandler. See ASR to "Dear Fannie," July 21 and Aug. 27, 1863, SRC-UCR. Chandler married William L. Candler in Aug. 1862, and Ropes hereafter refers to her as Fannie Candler.

34. ASR to EER, Aug. 2, 1862, SRC-UCR. Edward Ropes was with the 3d Brigade, 1st Division, 2d Army Corps, Army of Virginia. Dyer, *Compenium,* III, 1248.

however, were of little moment in light of national difficulties proceeding from the Seven Days experience. McClellan had failed to take Richmond, the Confederates remained in firm control of much of their territory, and Lincoln was urged to take immediate corrective measures.

The President's decisions involved significant alteration of the army command structure. McClellan's forces were withdrawn to the Washington area and reassigned to aid the new Army of Virginia, under Major General John Pope. Pope's contingent also included the forces of John C. Frémont, Nathaniel P. Banks, and Irvin McDowell. Henry W. Halleck was elevated to the position of general-in-chief of the Union armies, while "Little Mac" was ordered to support Pope.

Lincoln was worried about the safety of Washington, and his apprehensions were increased by Pope's inability to effectively subdue his rebel antagonists. On August 9, 1862, Thomas J. ("Stonewall") Jackson struck Banks's troops at Cedar Mountain and inflicted heavy losses on the Federal forces. Hannah Ropes was concerned for the safety of her son, who saw action with the Second Massachusetts regiment in this conflict, which resulted in 2,381 killed, missing, or wounded.[35] Jackson next moved north, to assail Pope's rear, while J.E.B. Stuart's cavalry attacked Union forces at Manassas. Pope failed to entrap the detached enemy contingent and Jackson managed to rejoin Robert E. Lee's army and prepare for the Second Battle of Bull Run, or Second Manassas.

Skirmishes leading to the main engagement of August 29-30 commenced on August 26 and were in full swing by the following day. Fears for the safety of Washington gripped the capital city. Rumors spread that Lee would soon enter the town, that Pope had suffered complete defeat, and that it was impossible to save Washington.[36] Conditions were not so bad as feared, but Second Manassas was nevertheless a serious defeat for Union fortunes. Pope's army retreated toward Washington, Lincoln puzzled over the problem of effective military command, and Confederate forces seemed invincible under the leadership of Lee and Jackson. Hannah Ropes,

---

35. Long and Long, *The Civil War Day by Day,* 249–50.
36. Ibid., 255–56; George B. McClellan, *McClellan's Own Story* (New York: Charles L. Webster, 1887), 530–35.

in the meantime, advised her daughter against coming to the troubled capital, and comforted the victims of rebel effectiveness.

ֲ‍

August, 1862
[No Date]

My Dear Alice,

. . . It is my opinion [that] you would be vastly happier to pass the winter with the Barnards than to open a school, and I advise you to go there.[37] I have asked Miss Stevenson and she says go by all means, because you would not go as a dependent, but on the contrary be precisely what they want in the family. The daughter who died such a shocking death was a pupil of Miss Stevenson and she says you can in a degree make good her place. If you were in a school, or I needed you here, it would be hard for you to break up, but if you were there a telegraph could send you on. Now, it would not do for you to be here. It is no place for young girls. The surgeons are young and look upon nurses as their natural prey.[38] We have been fortunate, but Dr. Hays, of whom I wrote, leaves next week for a fort near San Francisco.[39]

Wounded men are exposed from head to foot before the nurses and they object to anybody but an "old mother." This

37. George M. Barnard was a Boston merchant. He and his wife, Susan, had asked Alice Ropes to live with them for the winter. See Federal Census for 1860, Boston, Ward 6, George M. Barnard household, M653–521, FRC.

38. Youth was a characteristic among surgeons during the war. Surgeon General William A. Hammond, for example, was only 34 when appointed to his position in 1862. William Watson, a surgeon with the 105th Penn. Volunteer Regiment, held the rank of major at the age of 25. See William Watson, *Letters of a Civil War Surgeon,* ed. Paul Fatout (Lafayette, Ind.: Purdue Research Foundation, 1961), 11.

39. This was Acting Assistant Surgeon William W. Hays, who served in Union Hospital from June 17 to Aug. 17, 1862. Other medical personnel included James F. Kennedy, surgeon-in-charge, Acting Assistant Surgeon Charles W. Carrier, and Medical Cadets Edward Curtis, Henry S. Hannen, and R. H. Longwill. IMO-NA.

is not all. I don't like the tone of anything here. Refinement is not the order of society; still, I have thought something might arise to place it within my reach to have you come here if I stay, but even our remaining here is quite uncertain, as the government [officials] have to pay a heavy rent for the place and are fitting up cheap barracks of their own for hospital uses. I should feel perfectly easy about you with the Barnards, and could send for you with impunity. . . . I want you to go on with German and music if you have leisure. The German would be invaluable to me now, among the men.

I hope you write to Ned often. . . .

Your Mother

August, 1862
[No Date]

My dear Alice,

Yours, enclosing Ned's, is just received. Thanks. Wilson told me that any office Ned might desire he should have, if he could be found. If you can find out where to direct, do so at once. I did not ask this of Wilson, but he offered it. . . .

I do want Ned to have a commission and there is no trouble about it. I really think Wilson sent one to Kansas for him.[40]

I am sitting by Larh, who lost his hand.[41] He never kept still a moment, I believe, and it is awful hard to keep such a mercurial temperament from opening afresh the wound, and if it does again, the doctor says he must bleed to death. I have just told him I am a mind to throw him out of the window, and he says he wishes I would!

Our doctors are young but fine fellows. Close on the other

40. Edward Ropes did not want a commission because, as he told his grandmother, he did not feel qualified and had "seen too many deaths caused by inefficient officers." EPC to HAR, Nov. 19, 1862, and EER to ASR, Feb. 17, 1863, SRC-UCR.

41. This most likely was Pvt. J. Lahr, whose left forearm was removed by Acting Assistant Surgeon William W. Hays. See U.S. Surgeon General Office, *Medical and Surgical History*, II, Pt. 2, p. 989.

side is a man who has lost his foot. We have got them both on to water beds, and it is a great rest to them. The army is astir, and you may expect *news. We* look for patients every hour.

Your loving mother

H.A.R.

August 18, 1862
Union Hospital
Georgetown,
D.C.

My dear Neddie,
I am too thankful to receive yours of August 5th. Since then, there has been a fearful battle in which your regiment was terribly cut up, but as I do not see your name among the wounded I hope you are safe.[42]

I came here with a sister of J. Thomas Stevenson, of Boston, and Miss Kendall, of Plymouth, to attend the wounded soldiers. If General Banks would like us to come nearer his camp we are ready and anxious to go, or if anybody sick there will come here we will take the best care of them.[43]
. . .

I enclose the last news about Charlie.[44] I hope it will prove true, and he will recover; but with rebel care he will have a hard chance. If you ever get into that Sodom city, Richmond, I know you will find him if anybody can. Charlie Lyon has been very sick with fever on the Peninsula, unable to be

42. Ropes refers to the Battle of Cedar Mountain. Federal losses included 314 killed, 1,445 wounded, and 622 missing. Edward, with Nathaniel P. Banks's troops, saw some of the first fighting. Long and Long, *The Civil War Day by Day,* 249–50.

43. J. Thomas Stevenson was a prominent Boston merchant. His sister was Hannah E. Stevenson. See Federal Census for 1860, Boston, Ward 6, J. Thomas Stevenson household, M653–521, FRC. Nathaniel P. Banks, congressman and general from Massachusetts, commanded the 2d Army Corps, Army of Virginia.

44. Ropes enclosed a newspaper clipping indicating that Charles Peleg Chandler, her nephew, had been wounded but was still alive in a Richmond hospital.

moved.[45] Today's paper says the whole army have been moved from there and I hope to hear of him home, or at least brought here. Julia Sumner is here on a visit; [she] came with Charles to Washington on business. George is a hopeless paralytic and cannot step at all. Mrs. Sumner is better, . . . Alice [Ropes], they say, is looking finely. I hope she writes to you, because I get very little time.[46]

We have 200 beds here. The most of our men have recovered and gone back to their regiments—a few cripples remain. We have gained much praise for our care of them and hope to be filled up again soon. Come here if you get sick. Write me often.

Your Mother

August 27, 1862

Dear Alice,

Thanks for your kind and interesting letter from Ned and yourself. I wish you and Mrs. Gragg would get him up a box, and put in some wine, too. He is not strong enough to live under such a diet [as army fare]. You must look after him, and learn how he is to be reached. . . .

We are in the receipt of men from every division in the army and are expecting a rush of wounded today from Pope.[47] We have gone through twenty frights about Washington, and got so used to expecting to be taken

45. Charles Lyon Chandler, Ropes's nephew, was at this time a captain with the 34th Mass. Volunteer Infantry Regiment. See Mass. Adjutant General Office, *Record of the Massachusetts Volunteers,* II, 715.

46. Massachusetts Sen. Charles Sumner was the son of Charles P. and Relief Jacob Sumner, and was one of nine children. Julia Sumner was his youngest sister. His brother, George, a reformer in his own right, was stricken with paralysis and eventually died, on Oct. 6, 1863. See Edward L. Pierce, *Memoir and Letters of Charles Sumner,* 4 vols. (Boston: Roberts Brothers, 1877–93), I, 20, 31–34; IV, 97, 146, 169.

47. Maj. Gen. John Pope commanded the Army of Virginia. On Aug. 27, 1862, Union Hospital admitted 103 patients suffering from such maladies as dysentery, "debilitas," "icterus," constipation, lumbago, bronchitis, and ulcers. MR-NA.

prisoners that I think I am rather disappointed. The Massachusetts men of the 34th are nearly all ready to go to their regiments. I ran on to the steps and waved my handkerchief when the 35th went by, but I had no idea Dick Chute was among them. If I had, I should have stopped the regiment! Miss Boyce called for the second time for me to ride in an open carriage with two horses.[48] The country is beautiful but the roads [are] as bad as Pine Hill. . . .

. . . It made my heart ache to think of Ned. He ought to have a commission. Don't worry about Pope—his men here knew he meant to fall back, even to Manassas, as a decoy to the enemy and redeem that spot from last year's disgrace, while McClellan's army go in the rebels' rear, into Richmond.[49]

We have just cleaned and dressed over a hundred men from the Harrison's Landing—poor, worn fellows! The most of them are in the church opposite, which is under our supervision. . . .

Last week the Directors of Hospitals sent a committee out here to spy us out and take notes, because no other hospital had supported itself on government allowance. The Doctor took them into the kitchen and told the cook to tell them what we had for dinner and breakfast that day.[50] Then,

48. Richard Henry Chute, 2d Lieut. in the 59th Mass. Volunteer Infantry Regiment, was Ropes's nephew. See Mass. Adjutant General Office, *Record of the Massachusetts Volunteers,* II, 937. Bessie Boyce and her widowed mother, Mrs. M.M. Boyce, were Ropes's friends and lived on the heights overlooking Georgetown. Mrs. Boyce, "of the same family as the Earls of Montrose," had purchased the former Elderslie estate and named it "Montrose." Her rose gardens were apparently notable and "were always open to the public." *Washington, D.C.: A guide to the Nation's Capital,* American Guide Series (New York: Hastings House, 1942), 365–66. See also *Hutchinson's Washington and Georgetown Directory, 1863* (Washington, D.C.: Hutchinson & Bro., 1863), 221, and Andrew Boyd, *Boyd's Washington and Georgetown Directory, 1864* (Washington, D.C.: Hudson Taylor, 1863), 295.

49. For typical historical opinion contradicting this view, see Eisenschiml., *The Celebrated Case of Fitz-John Porter,* 49–56.

50. The physician to whom Ropes refers was James F. Kennedy, assist-

upstairs, they questioned patients in every ward, and were told they had everything they wanted. You may imagine the surprise of the committee at this, but you can't when we assured them that we had over four hundred dollars over of ration money at the end of each month from which we bought some water beds, subscribed for twenty daily papers, the two monthlies, and place[d] the rest in the hospital fund![51] This hospital was pronounced a *"Model Hospital."*

I enclose a measure for a pair of tie shoes and a pair of boots for little Mrs. Warren, who is our needle woman, . . .[52] If anybody offers to get anything for me, let them; or, if they wish to send some money to me, I shall be very glad, and not ashamed to take it. . . . I miss you and mother very much, but I can't go back unless you need me more than the soldiers do. I am going to ride with Miss Boyce at five o'clock. . . . Don't worry if you hear the enemy are driving our men into Washington—they will find their way back closed forever! But there is to be *no peace* till Freedom for all.

Your Mother

• Despite Ropes's enthusiasm, Union fortunes in early September 1862 seemed to be declining. Disruption in the high command and apprehensions concerning possible foreign recognition of the Confederate States made an important victory essential. From Richmond, on the other hand, the perspective seemed optimistic. A notable victory now might destroy the already damaged Federal morale and bring peace with independence. Accordingly, Robert E. Lee received permission from rebel authorities to invade the North. Crossing the Potomac on September 5, his forces moved into Maryland, creating fears in the United States regarding the

---

ant surgeon, U.S. Army, who was in charge of Union Hospital from July 16 to Sept. 16, 1862. IMO-NA.

51. Union Hospital apparently had ample food for the patients, and government food allowances seem to have been normally generous. See Leech, *Reveille in Washington,* 223, and Woolsey, *Hospital Days,* 30.

52. This was Mrs. P.H. Warren, a volunteer nurse, also listed on the hospital muster rolls as "Fannie Warren." MR-NA.

possible fall of such places as Baltimore and Washington. Rebel success at Harper's Ferry and elsewhere sharpened Northern anxiety, and this was further whetted by McClellan's apparent slowness in responding to the Southern threat.

Although "Little Mac" had numerical troop superiority and also a copy of Lee's orders, showing the position of Confederate forces, he moved cautiously and did not encounter the enemy until September 17, at the Battle of Antietam, or Sharpsburg, Maryland. This battle, the bloodiest of the war to that time, stopped Lee's advance. The Confederates, however, were able to return to Virginia, and McClellan received round criticism for failing to entrap and destroy them. Meanwhile, the wounded Union soldiers limped back to Washington to receive care in the army hospitals, and Hannah Ropes worked to alleviate their suffering.

[Apparently September 18–30, 1862]

My Dear Mother,

The box containing the shirt so nicely made came safely to me. I have shown the shirt to several of the nurses, but not yet have I seen the man I am willing to honor by dressing him in it. He will appear in due time. I have not found time to answer any letters for the past two weeks. The house has been full of suffering of such a complicated nature as you can hardly conceive. We have been up from six in the morning till one at night, and then laid down ready to jump at a moment's warning.

The young man who was shot through the lungs, to our surprise and, as the surgeons say, contrary to all "science," lived till last night, or rather this morning. We considered him the greatest sufferer in the house, as every breath was a pang. I laid down last night and got asleep, when I was roused by hearing him cry, very loud, "Mother! Mother! Mother!" I was out of bed and into my dressing gown very quickly, and by his side. The pressure of blood from the unequal circulation had affected the brain slightly, and, as they all are, he was on the battlefield, struggling to get away from the enemy. I promised him that nobody should touch him, and that in a few moments he would be free from all pain. He believed me and, fixing his beautiful eyes upon my face, he never turned them away; resistance, the resistance of a strong natural will, yielded; his breathing grew more gentle, ending softly as an infant's. He was a brave soldier and a truthful boy.

Last Sunday I left him for an hour to go into the church opposite and hear the service. It was an impressive sight. The church was full of beds, the chaplain stood near the entrance between the beds, and a few singers sat on stools behind him. The nurses were fanning the sickest patients; and near one bed sat the mother of the sick man. I think they all felt the better for the services. I only wore my cap and stood among the patients. Outside, the rumble of army wagons made almost indistinct the words of the speaker. The doctor told me yesterday that I must spend four hours outdoors. Today, upon the strength of such a charge, Miss Stevenson and I got into the horse cars and rode into Washington, up to the Capitol, winding round to the Depot. So shut into hospital life have we been that we never knew that we could go from our own door to the Depot from which we go home. We did not conclude to go just yet, but rode back as we went, having a nice bit of fresh air. I had a pleasant call from Mrs. Barnard and her two sons. She seemed delighted with Alice and very anxious to have her with them this winter. I hope you approve of the arrangement.[53]

I don't know how long we shall be able to hold out; we shall stay till longer stay would make us only a care to others. Our house is one of constant death now. Every day some one drops off the corruption of a torn and wounded body. It is more from the worn condition of the soldier before the wound, and the torture of exposure on the field, added to which a forced removal in heavy wagons to the hospitals, than to the dangerous nature of the wounds.[54]

53. Alice, having sold her mother's house, had been asked by Susan Barnard, wife of Boston merchant George M. Barnard, to live with the family. ASR to EER, Sept. 5, 1862, SRC-UCR.

54. For suffering of soldiers prior to arrival at the general hospitals, see

I wrote you a long letter which I hope you received. I have heard nothing from Ned lately. Our people are jubilant over the last victory.[55] As for old Dutch Pennsylvania, the farmers are at length touched where they can feel to the quick, namely their homes, and the uprising is truly amusing as well as wonderful.

I wish you would write to me. No one tells me half as much news as you do. I may be back to Thanksgiving, or on your birthday, for a visit if nothing more.

With love to all. Your loving child.

H.A.R.

October 6, 1862

Dear Alice,

. . . I literally have no time to myself, and write at a running pace—for instance, in writing the above, I have got up to attend to a man who has just had his leg taken off—he is reduced in strength, and it always is a good deal of a job to bring a weak man safe out from the effect of the chloroform.[56] The doctors say give all the brandy they will take, but be sure and keep them awake.

Today we send off fifty men. Not half of them are able to go, but that is of no account to one head surgeon, who cares no more for a private than for a dog.[57] Dr. Hays was a prince of a youth; but he would marry, and so had to go away. We upon the whole have had goodish men to rule over us. Still, between surgeons, stewards, nurses and waiters, the poor men in all the hospitals barely escape with life or clothes or money.

Bell Irvin Wiley, *The Life of Billy Yank: The Common Soldier of the Union* (Indianapolis: Bobbs-Merrill, 1952), 144.

55. The Battle of Antietam, Sept. 17, 1862.

56. Death from chloroform was possible, even in stronger patients. See U.S. Surgeon General Office, *Medical and Surgical History,* II, Pt. 3, pp. 890–94.

57. This was A.M. Clark, assistant surgeon, U.S. Volunteers, who was in charge of Union Hospital from Sept. 16 to Nov. 8, 1862. IMO-NA.

The wars on James River [are] nothing compared with the fights I have with the stewards. We now have our fourth, as big a villain as ever walked unhung.[58] I have entered a complaint to the Surgeon General but I don't suppose it will do any good at all. But at any rate I shall have nothing to do with him. I ordered him out of my room, and don't speak to him now. The men have not had enough to eat for a week—this morning, one slice of bread to each man! As soon as I found it out, I took a half bushel of apples and went into the court and told the men if I could have my way they should have more than enough, and I hoped the steward would go hungry sometime. They gathered round me as thick as chickens and [ate] their apples. It was all I had from a barrel sent me.[59] Tell the country people to dry all the apples they can for the soldiers.

I have stopped again, Alice, to close the eyes of a gentle German boy who has no one in this country to mourn for him. His parents live in the father land, and all the record there will be is a number on his grave.[60]

I hear nothing from Ned and very little war news. Everything is hush here and the wants of the soldiers fill all minds with whom I come in contact. I hope you will be very happy at Mrs. Barnard's. I think you the best of company, and I am not surprised that she is of that opinion too.

Your Mother

• The fall of 1862 was busy for those serving in the Washington hospitals. Besides her nursing duties, Ropes had much to think

58. Troubles with stewards were common. This was Henry Perkins, who served in Union Hospital from Aug. 31 to Oct. 31, 1862. The muster roll for that quarter contains "Remarks" after his name which say, "Under arrest by Order Sec. War; pay & clothing due from date of enlistment." MR-NA.

59. Ropes's concern for her patients was known and appreciated by their relatives. See David Jenkins to Dr. J. Winslow, Sept. 21, 1862; Katie Hoff to Edward Hoff, Oct. 5, 1862; Abigail Taft to Henry Snyder and HAR, Oct. 18, 1862; Katie Hoff to "Dear Lady," Oct. 27, 1862, SRC-UCR.

60. This was Charles Hauser, corporal, F Co., 45th N.Y. Volunteers.

about with regard to the actions of the steward and head surgeon. Caring for the sick and wounded soldiers was difficult enough under the best of circumstances, but now normal problems were complicated by what she believed were dubious deeds of unfeeling administrators. Relating this in letters to others, she now commenced a diary—which she hoped subsequently to publish, as she had her letters from Kansas—and recorded therein her now growing worries.

October [1–9], 1862.

New days bring new trials to combat; and, while we are cheered with the prospective recovery of most of those brought in after the battles in which General Pope's command was engaged, we turn away with saddened eyes from the long list of those whose last sleep has fallen upon them in this hospital. Fifteen have died within the month just ended, some of them so worn out with fatigue and fasting as to be wholly unable to rally, others kept along with wounded limbs until too exhausted to bear amputation, and thus died. It would be folly to say they all might have lived with more prompt attention; it is also unjust to a true conviction not to say they have lost their only chance through a lack of earnest interest in the superior surgeon.[61] Apothecary and medicine chest might be dispensed with if an equal amount of genuine sympathy could be brought home to our stricken men and the rations be converted into more delicate food.[62] Not more than eight cents per day is the cost actually dealt out by the steward! Our men have been saved only by the best of nurses and the kind and constant help from friends at home; and to those good people we turn our eyes, as the fainting

---

Admitted to Union Hospital on Sept. 25, 1862, he died of "dysentara" on Oct. 6, 1862. MR-NA.

61. Ropes refers to A.M. Clark, the surgeon-in-charge.

62. Others also emphasized the patients' need for friendship and personal concern. See Alcott, *Hospital Sketches,* 34, and Whitman, *The Wound Dresser,* 14, 44–45.

mariner throws his glance across the dreary distance of ocean towards some approaching sail.[63]

This steward I think will prove the climax of unfaithful servants. Indeed they are a strange race of mortals, so far as I have watched them; and, as we have had four during our hospital life of three months, perhaps I am as well prepared to judge them as others. Our first was a *Jew*—round faced, beady eyes, black hair and short of stature. He would talk so sweet to me, and rob me of a bottle of wine, a shirt or pretty pocket handkerchief at the very moment I was looking at him to reply! It was the kind will of providence that this spawn of the reptile species should be sent to the Peninsula, after ushering into his place a gentle, well disposed Pennsylvanian, who knew about as much of the world and society as his neighboring Dutch farmers, of the present President. He soon grew tired of the annoyances of his position and was transferred. Number 3 was from Virginia, young, compact, becoming his uniform remarkably well; but his features all turned up and his manner suggested to me the nature of a porcupine.

He thrust his quills at everybody and the waters of our earnest but harmonious life were terribly troubled. I kept out of his way till he came to my premises. Then we had a pitched battle over the rights of the soldiers, lasting a good hour. At the close, he hauled down his colors, took a cup of hot tea from my hand, and we laid some plans for bettering the diet of the patients.

In a few days he was transferred to another hospital. When he came to tell me I told him I was *really sorry,* for I had become reconciled to him, and took him to be honest at

63. Gifts to patients from friends and relatives at home were valuable in supplementing hospital fare and improving patient morale. Nurses requested that such items as beef extract, brandy, shirts, flannel drawers, pocket handkerchiefs, towels, and nutmegs be sent; and gifts ranged widely, from pickles and wines to books, puzzles, and woolen socks. See Woolsey, *Hospital Days,* 53–55, and Wormeley, *The Other Side of the War,* 91.

heart, and not to blame for being born under the influence of slavery. We parted friends, and in kindness. Our next and last, a French Canadian, came in with the doubtful, dreary sphere of a raven or a bat. Dressed in his dark blue suit of pants and close fitting jacket, with a wide, bright green stripe down the side, and making a cuff to the sleeve above the elbow, a stiff linen collar up under his ears, and both hands thrust down into his pockets, we felt that this man was the opener of a new epoch.

The head surgeon was also a new man, tall, stiff, thin, light hair, whity blue eyes, and whity yellow complexion, glasses on eyes, and a way of looking out at the end of his glasses at you, surreptitiously, if I may use so big a word. He was young and I took to him. He was ignorant of hospital routine; ignorant of life outside of the practice in a country town, in an interior state, a weak man with good intentions, but puffed up with the gilding on his shoulder straps. If he had not been weak, and it had been my style to make a joke at the expense of others, there was a fine chance here; but he was safe at my hands, for he *was* weak, and I am strong in the knowledge at least which comes with age. And it is likely that in some way even this man, made giddy with an epaulette, will learn that God has made the private and officer of one equality, so far as the moral treatment of each other is concerned.

October 10, 1862.

I have tonight packed up soup, towels, brandy, sandwiches and crackers for Dr. Clark to take with him out to the battlefield of Antietam—he goes with many others; it is a dark and rainy night. I have put into his hands and Dr. Kennedy's fresh stockings for their comfort, in case they get wet feet. I really wanted to go with them, but I cannot leave my post here.

Dr. Ottman is in charge in the absence of Dr. Clark. I think he is a fine example of a Christian gentleman. He is a quiet, well balanced, and self contained person, of small stature and open face; we all took to him as soon as he appeared. And

Miss Stevenson, in whose ward he is, thinks much of his medical skill.[64]

October 11, 1862.

The new steward has been in to my room to talk about the washing. I show him how badly the clothes are washed.[65] I did not know till after he left the room that he kept back a part of the ration of soap. I think the hardest thing for me to comprehend is such meanness.

He seemed to be trying to buy me, and I was involuntarily getting at the quality of his mind; he spoke rather contemptuously of the privates. I fired up at that and told him, "they were really the heroes of the war, that there were privates in the house who were independent so far as money makes men so, and they knew what their rights were as privates." He said, with a sneer, he was not of the benevolent kind, that he was here to make all the money he could out of the hospital, adding triumphantly that the power was in his hands, that he had sent away three loads of their clothes now! As for his rude manners to myself, I record no charge; not considering him my equal, there can be no personal contest between us. "We do not gather grapes of thorns." The time left to any of us after half a century is but short at best. I am here to do my Master's work; the poor privates are my special children for the present; I never wash their hard, worn, and sore feet without a sweet memory of Him who gave us the example; I never see them wronged, or neglected, or in want, without the feeling that every drop of my blood would be well spent if it could make up to them a tithe of the loss they have experienced in health, in spirits, in weakened faith in man, as well as shattered hope in themselves![66]

64. The physicians to whom Ropes refers were A.M. Clark, James F. Kennedy (apparently—hospital muster rolls only indicate his presence to Sept. 16, 1862), and R. Ottman, acting assistant surgeon. IMO-NA.

65. Union Hospital maintained a staff of laundresses to wash the patients' clothing. MR-NA.

66. The plight of the common soldier in the military hospitals was

As the true life of this steward gleamed upon me, astonishment took the place of all other emotions. When I first began to think, standing there before him, I found I had received from him the impression that we could work together in the game of peculation! Then I said, "You may go, I think I have your measure now." In the space of an hour he came back to the door and knocked. Suspecting who it was, I said to Fanny [Warren], the needle woman, "I will open the door, for I think it is the steward," and so it was. He made a most gracious bow; I stepped onto the threshold and said, "No farther sir! Neither now nor at any other time—go your way and I mine, they are wide apart."

Every day the inmates of the house bring charges against him to me; I have been to the head surgeon but it makes not the slightest impression upon him. I wrote to the "Surgeon General" [but] the letter came back to the "Surgeon in Charge," whereupon the last named functionary, living in the same house, sent a formal "official notice" to me that I must prove the grave charges made against the steward![67] As though I had not better business to do than to dabble in such muddy water! I only reiterated my belief in his dishonesty and declined to hunt for evidence which was plain in the kitchen, the larder, and every pinched face one meets on the stairs or in the wards.

• Surgeon General William A. Hammond's referral of Ropes's letter to A.M. Clark, the chief hospital surgeon, accorded with military procedure, which called for communication with higher authorities only through the chain-of-command. Having spoken first with Clark, however, Ropes believed that remedial action could only be obtained by approaching Hammond directly—an illusion which was quickly dispelled.

Ropes's letter may have seemed to Hammond simply a routine matter which merited staff attention rather than his own. Or, his

bemoaned by many. According to Walt Whitman, "everybody seems to try to pick upon them." *The Wound Dresser,* 159.

67. Ropes refers to Surgeon General William A. Hammond.

action may well have been due to an all-too-frequent tendency on the part of women nurses to criticize hospital administrators and procedures, which produced a predictable defensiveness in medical authorities and often caused them to view nurses' statements as carping rather than as valid complaints. If the latter was the case, Ropes's reply to Clark's demand that she detail her charges did little to change matters. A woman's intuition—upon which she placed so much importance—and reported conversations were insufficient evidence to justify corrective action by the chief surgeon. And that she had approached his superiors on the matter without his knowledge could hardly have made her a welcome plaintiff. Still, her record as a dependable nurse might logically have made her statements grounds for a possible internal investigation. But Clark's mind, for whatever reason, was closed against Ropes—a fact he would soon have cause to regret—and he ignored her complaint. Here is the text of the letter Ropes submitted to the chief surgeon:

Dear Sir,
Your "official Document" was rather a surprise, on two counts; first, that a lady could not express an honest opinion either by note or word of mouth without its passing out from the hand or the ear receiving it; and secondly, that she should be expected or rather compelled to give a *reason* for her honest opinion.
Of the dishonesty of the steward, I have no [manner] of doubt. To prove him so would be dabbling in dirtier water than I care to touch and take time which I came here to spend otherwise.
How I came to judge him as I have is through two channels, one a woman's intuitions, which if she lives an orderly life are as unerring as the finger of God, and as such, God forbid that she should fail to follow—the other, his own words to me and to his clerk.
In my room, while contending with him for food suitable for the men, he said with a sneer he was not of the benevolent kind, that his business was to make all the money he could out of the hospital, adding triumphantly that the power was in his hands. If the sick privates had been dogs, he could not have spoken more contemptuously of them. In the course of his remarks, he said he had sent three loads of their clothes away from the house, and he had a right to do so.
Now I happen to know that [many of these clothes] were

perfectly whole and clean, and all the poor fellows owned. I have taxed myself and my friends to the utmost to make good to them their loss.

For the facts stated to me by the clerk, you have him to refer to. And as for his rude manner to myself, I bring no charge. Not considering him my equal, there can be no personal contest between us.

"We do not gather grapes of thorns." In regard to the course I have taken in uttering such "grave charges" I have but one *personal rule,* and that is never to speak in self defense. Among my own people, 50 years of my life is on record, the time left to anyone after that is very short at best. I am here doing my Master's work. The poor privates are my children for the time being. . . .

October 24, 1862.

Rode down to the Depot with Miss Stevenson, saw her into the car with her face set towards her home—that land of rugged hills, poor soil, and hard work; that country of freedom to think, to speak and to act; that place of clean water, clean linen, and clean houses; where the men can read and write, and the women make a Christian shirt and knit a pair of stockings that will come within a finger's length of a common civilized foot!

That dear lady did not know how badly I felt at parting with her! I ran out of the car to shake off the gathering emotion!

Had we not worked together, an uphill struggle, for four months? And even as she went, did I not know as well, and perhaps better, than she that she had succumbed to the pressure of opposing spheres in our work, and improper food? Thanks to the good old Bay State that old veterans in this war, like us, can go back feeling sure of a welcome, and plenty in the "basket and in the store."

The steward has turned the screws a little tighter, not so much because Miss Stevenson has gone as because there followed in her wake that sweet little "red riding hood" from

New Hampshire who nestled under her wing on the ward; and who feared the steward too much to stay without her presence. The boys are all in tears; one on crutches has come to sit in my room, as the nearest approximation to his faithful nurses.

Dr. Hinkle has a relapse of fever at Mrs. Boyce's. I try to forget the loneliness of my room by going to see him.[68]

He knows all our trials here. He came to us early in September with another physician from Philadelphia, when our needs were great, the house being full of wounded men. I met them at the foot of the staircase that morning and they told me their errand, asking where they should begin. I took them up to the ward of Miss Stevenson, for I liked to have men on stretchers taken up to her, feeling sure it was the greatest kindness I could do them.

Over the bed of a man with a bullet in his thigh I shook hands with Dr. Hinkle. How gentle he was to the suffering soldier; and how vigorously he worked to relieve him! Looking up full in his face at the first breathing spell, I was struck with his paleness, as well as the beauty of his manner—my first *St. John* among the surgeons!

But now it seems almost impossible that he should rally, so exhausted did he become in the zeal of his labors for the month of September.

Is it that the multitude of men, passing into the world of spirits through the fierce passions of a violent death, need such as he to soothe and help them, that he also must fling off his present field of labor and accept a "transfer?"

• Ropes's concerns regarding the actions of the steward continued to grow. Thwarted by Hammond and Clark in attempts to remedy the situation through recourse to the medical department, she became more inclined to take her complaints to other authorities. She described her actions in a letter to her daughter.

68. This was A.G.B. Hinkle, of Philadelphia. See U.S. Surgeon General Office, *Medical and Surgical History*, II, Pt. 2, p. 358.

October 25, 1862

Dear Alice,

I saw Fanny yesterday and she had not heard anything more from home than I have, so we consoled each other with the belief that you were all well.[69]

Her views of Washington coincide with mine; I believe she has not yet seen any female whom she considered worth speaking to. But as the streets and hotels are thronged with officers, she has a chance to judge something about them. I think she is very happy.

Your letter from Chelsea has arrived, and also Fanny. I hoped by this time you were at the Barnards', as they were expecting you. Write me all about it when you get settled there. Their son was wounded in the hand. Did he go home? There are two boxes marked for him and landed here, with a cargo from Harrison's Landing. If Mr. Barnard will send me an order for them, I will have them brought here and opened, as the contents may spoil. Don't send anything to me unless someone is coming on, or somebody sends a box to me. The steward and I have not finished up yet—he struck a boy with a chisel and put him in the guard house.

He did not know that even women could send telegraphs, and was rather taken aback the next morning when the father of the boy arrived from Philadelphia before breakfast and demanded the boy! Before night a man came in and asked what he put him in there for. The steward said with an oath, "It is none of your business." The man passed up the stairs into the ward and saw the boy's roommate, asked for the name of the steward and head surgeon, wrote it down with a pencil, and in thrusting it into his pocket his shabby coat fell open, revealing a *General's strap!* Last night General Banks arrived; he asked for me—the cup of chagrin to the steward seemed full![70]

69. Frances Vaughan Chandler, Ropes's relative, was married on Aug. 19, 1862, to Capt. William L. Candler.

70. Nathaniel P. Banks at this time was in charge of the defenses of Washington, D.C.

Banks looks old and thin—said he would come again. I am
going to ride up to Mrs. Boyce's to dine at four o'clock.
Bessie will call for me, so I will close—write often—

Your mother

H.A.R.

• It was doubtless some comfort to Ropes that her longtime
friend, Nathaniel P. Banks, was now in charge of Washington's
defenses, and his presence in the hospital to visit her could hardly
have escaped the notice of the steward and head surgeon. Her
conflict with the hospital authorities, together with the effort of
caring for her patients, placed great stress on the Massachusetts
matron, and this worried her mother, at home. Esther Parsons
Chandler wrote her daughter on October 29, 1862, saying that "I
am willing you should be usefuley imployed in takeing care of the
sick & wounded," but "It distresses me to have you want for the
comforts of life. You may injure your health perminantly. Why not
petition for the removal of the steward [?]" Discussing some news
from home, she admonished Ropes not to "stay there till you get
starved out" and to "write son and let us know if you have made a
change for the beter."

Ropes, however, was neither about to return home nor cease her
efforts in behalf of the patients. The national cause for which she
was laboring was still very much in doubt. The Battle of Antietam
had been only a momentary repulse for the rebels, whose morale
was in the ascendant, and J.E.B. Stuart's raid around McClellan's
entire army, from October 10–12, which took him as far north as
Chambersburg, Pennsylvania, only increased Union embarassment.
By early November, prodded by Lincoln, McClellan had
crossed the Potomac in preparation for a move on Richmond. But
shortly thereafter the Railsplitter relieved "Little Mac" of command
and replaced him with Major General Ambrose E. Burnside.
Discontent among the troops—generally loyal to McClellan—and
the renewed halt in Union progress emphasized the history of
Federal difficulties. While national efforts proceeded uneasily, so
did those at Union Hospital. But while the first would take several
months to resolve, those facing Hannah Ropes were now brought
to a crisis and solution, and the matron recorded the events in her
hospital diary.

November 1, 1862.

This month, generally so sombre as it turns to face us,
appears in the triple adornment of August warmth without
its dryness, July brightness of sky without its fierceness of
heat, and the calm repose of matronly June, when she
hopefully lets fall the blossom petals of her bridal morning
and sits waiting "her fullness of time."

Our hospital life approaches the current where breakers,
long known, appear in full view. Today the steward's reign
reaches a culminating point. I had said yesterday to Dr.
Ottman, in his room, "Do you know a *dark hole* has been
parted off in the cellar, said to be for any patient the steward
chooses to incarcerate therein?"

The chaplain was in the room at the time, a gentle refugee
from Virginia and a professor in some college there.
Peaceful, retired citizens both, neither answered directly.
The question was incidental, after I had closed the object of
my call. I rose from my chair to leave, but turned, placing my
hands on the back of my chair, looking askingly at them both.
I said, "You men may have fears too strong to allow you to
act, I have no office to lose or gain. I am free to do right, and if
any patient in this house is put into that black hole I will go to
Washington and stay till I gain the 'open sessame' to that
door. How can you let this hospital be turned into a prison?"
This was all in the most unbroken good humor, and the
chaplain, smiling, said, "I am afraid, Mrs. Ropes, you are not
altogether orthodox on this point of discipline." [Ropes:]
"Well, no, I doubt if I am." [Chaplain:] "Suppose now, one of
the men goes out on a 'pass' and comes home intoxicated?"

[Ropes:] "I think, sir, the best use I can make of him would
be to put him into a good warm bed and give him to drink a
cup of strong, hot coffee!" We all laughed and I came down
the long corridors musing, as I passed the beds of my boys,
upon the price we pay to save a race which hardly seems
worth the saving. It was eleven o'clock and the stir for dinner
preparation began as I finished my rounds and slumped into

my chair to look at the morning paper. The door into the clothes room stood wide open, and hardly was I seated with spectacles on my nose before Fanny [Warren] appeared, pale and trembling, holding by the door. "Mrs. Ropes! Julius is in that awful place!" "What! In the cellar?" "Yes, what shall we do?" "Do!" Off went the glasses, down went the paper, away broke my prospective rest of half an hour in my easy chair; and when I had tumbled noisily out of that chair another figure apppeared in the door by Fanny's side—our little mite of a Miss Kendall. With the purpose of a total self abnegation written all over every day of our four months life here, she was not the person to look on and see so gross a wrong; no! And as I caught sight of her quivering face, her earnest, sad eyes, glistening with tears that drift and float there always, and after contesting the premises with bright and merry glances of joy and satisfaction over the thing that is right, I said, "Come, will you go with me?"

"Yes, I'm sure I will go anywhere if there is the slightest prospect of redress; I see how utterly impossible it has become to sit idle any longer."

Our bonnets were soon on, and we in the car. Our first call was at General Banks' headquarters: He had gone to New York! Then we went to find Fanny Candler, so as to enlist her husband into going with us unto the center of governing power; for be it known to you all, it is not a pretty pleasure excursion to thrust oneself into the business hiding places of persons in power; it was only the amount of outside pressure in the shape of that cell under my room which brought me up to it, and even with that I was ready to catch at any hand of the stronger sex who would help me over this unpleasant piece of duty.

The fates were cruel and stern in leaving us no aider but ourselves. Fanny's rooms were closed. Major Ladd had started for home. We took a car back to the Surgeon General's office. Three chairs lined the side of the public entrance; two strong men held up, respectively, the side of the door and the rail of the stairs. I asked audience of the

Surgeon General; the man at the door post said, "It is three o'clock, and he is never here after that time." As he spoke, the Surgeon walked in and, passing us without the Christian courtesy of a look or a nod, or even the old time civility of raising the hand to his hat, he vanished behind the opening door of his inner office.

Rather tired, but with unfailing purpose, we sat down in the stiff wooden chairs gracing this public thoroughfare, to consider. There was a dreadful weight at my heart; to help the oppressed did not seem at all the sphere of this place where we sat. That broad built piece of humanity with gilded straps, with a stomach made extensively capacious by much good living—what had it in common with my poor, half starved soldiers? Ah! It seemed like trying to lift off Atlas on one's back, this bringing justice and mercy to kiss each other. The man at the staircase followed his master, then came back to ask if I could send in my message. "No, it must be given in by myself." He returned only to say we could see the Assistant Surgeon, but at his door in the rear of the entry we were met with the notice that we must wait, he was engaged.

Two rebuffs seemed about enough for a woman of half a century to accept without compromising her own dignity, and answered too as sufficient spur to take us to the Secretary of War office.

• Ropes's impatience with Surgeon General Hammond was doubtless due in some degree to his treatment of her previous complaints concerning Union Hospital. His remanding her earlier missive to A.M. Clark had caused her frustration and embarrassment, and it is unlikely that she would have taken umbrage so readily in the present situation had this not occurred. Hammond's former action and Clark's arbitrary handling of Ropes's grievances now bore bitter fruit, for she took her case directly to Edwin M. Stanton, whose dislike for Hammond was well established. The secretary of war was ready to investigate any error for which a "McClellan man," such as Hammond, was responsible. Ropes, therefore, wittingly or not, gave Stanton an opportunity to take direct action in a situation which technically came under the cognizance of the surgeon general. A woman unused to the restraints of bureaucracy, she acted to accomplish her ends in the most direct manner available, and did not care in the slightest for the "propriety" involved. Stanton, on the other hand, although Hammond's superior, ignored the surgeon general's position and prerogatives, which as secretary of war he might have been expected to uphold. Fortunately for the patients at Union Hospital, neither Ropes nor Stanton felt bound by the chain-of-command. In Ropes's case, the intention proceeded from a desire to help her patients. In Stanton's, however, political factors must rank as at least a partial rationale—a fact witnessed by Hammond's attempt to save Clark from the secretary's punishment (see diary entry of November 8, 1862, below). But whatever Stanton's motives, Ropes was pleased by her reception at his office—and its results.

[*November 1, 1862,* diary entry continues]

Here the tone of things was very much more genial; we were welcomed at least as having a right to sit in a nice room, and received the promise of seeing the Secretary as soon as he came to his room. Ten minutes passed, during which I kept my eyes on the floor while I counted out what I should wear in case I had to sit down cellar with Julius all night. For Fanny [Warren] I had sent down to listen at the door, and she heard the young German sobbing and praying to God not to forsake him, for he had no father, no mother, and no friends in this country, and she whispered to him through the keyhole, "Cheer up, Mrs. Ropes is going to befriend you now." Just as I had completed my imaginary equipments for a night as guard to a prison door, among the rats and cockroaches, a large man with dark beard, bald head, and legal brow walked into the room, stationing himself in front of a desk. The gentleman who had so kindly greeted us when we came, told me who it was. I went to the end of the desk and, without introducing myself at all, stated in the fewest words possible the facts about Julius. Secretary Stanton's eyes gleamed with the fire of a purpose.

"Call the Provost Marshal" was all he said, and went on

writing.[71] Before we got hold of the importance of the order, that functionary appeared. Stanton lifted the pen from the paper and, looking at him, said, "Go to the Union Hospital with this lady, take the boy out of that black hole, go into it yourself so as to be able to tell me all about it, then arrest the steward and take him to a cell in the Old Capitol Prison, to await further orders!"

Very soberly he said it, and as soberly he said to me, "I am very much obliged to you, very much, for giving me this information."[72]

Two lighter hearted creatures than Miss Kendall and myself could not be found. The same car that brought us out, brought the men to take away our ogre, the steward. It was a frightfully grand scene to see the maze of the steward, the joy of the men, and pale terror of the head surgeon.

The under officers were particularly in fear, such as cooks, waiters, and clerks. More or less, according to the balancing strength of the parties, the steward had bought them over, and having considerable wholesome respect for the government, [and] some knowledge of the fact that they had not been true quite to the interests of the men, there was much quaking in their shoes.

November 4, 1862.

A whole lifetime has been crowded into the past four days. Straps and buttons have been hurrying through the halls; wise looking men in long boots have stood about; and legal people have been into my rooms to take testimony. Above everything else, the head surgeon has been spirited off and locked in the Old Capitol Prison.[73] As I have said before, I say now, he is the

71. This was apparently Lafayette C. Baker, who was appointed special provost marshal for the War Department in Sept. 1862.

72. Stanton appears in general to have been kindly disposed toward women nurses. See Livermore, *My Story of the War,* 271–72, and Hancock, *South After Gettysburg,* 48.

73. Noah Brooks referred to this prison as "that maloderous Bastille." *Washington, D.C., in Lincoln's Time,* 66.

dupe of a strong and wicked man [the steward]. That he would be very angry with me I have expected. Perhaps Stanton had the same expectation when he sent an "Official Order" for the head surgeon *not* to remove me from my place in this hospital. The lawyer who came to take testimony had whispered to me that a request had been made to have me removed, and that Stanton indignantly replied, "It shall not be done." Somehow, the fact did not wound me; why should it, when the question, "Why do the surgeons, from the general to his humblest aides, feel so sensitive about this matter," remains unanswered? Certainly one would suppose the opening up of any iniquity like this would be looked upon and hailed by all as the best possible good a motherly woman could do. Let that be as it will, if I was to live that day over again I could not do differently.

On Saturday the Medical Inspector came to look about.[74] I had been sent for an hour previous to go in with one of the nurses and Julius to the War Department. A nice carriage came for us; the visit did not amount to much because we were sent for to return and give evidence to the Inspector.

This man I had seen here with Governor Andrew—a large man with heavy gray beard, clear blue eyes, thoughtful mien, and a cautious tongue.[75] Then the full, bald head—what a sheet anchor in a storm! He came in and sat down by me in a fatherly way, and I could have told him everything I ever did without a doubt of justice at his hands. First he asked me about the steward, and I stated all I could remember of his conversations up to the time when I said, "Mr. Steward, I think I have your measure now; you may go, and don't ever put your foot over my threshold again!"

All the time these clear blue eyes were looking calmly into my face. There came a half suppressed smile over his face, but it faded and the judge only was visible. Then he asked me

74. This was Medical Inspector General Thomas F. Perley, appointed in April 1862. See Adams, *Doctors in Blue,* 40.
75. Ropes refers to Gov. John A. Andrew, of Massachusetts.

about the Doctor. I replied truthfully, but also with a leaning towards pity. I remembered his wife, his future and, yes, his vanity. It seemed as though he could never rise above so heavy a disgrace as a discharge from the service; and I said, "He is a nervous, irritable person; the work here has been new to him, and he is young, too young for the place; beside, his past life has given him no general knowledge of society. Then there are two points of attack upon him where he has been weak; first, in the bad influence of the steward, who is really the strongest mind of the two, and who, Faust-like, whispers ever in his ear thoughts of evil; the second is the majesty of his shoulder straps. They seem to have conveyed to his mind a sense of irresponsible power."

"But," said the Inspector, "you believe him unjust to the patients."

"Yes indeed, always harsh and unsympathizing, but you can see as well as I that it will not mend the matter to punish him any more than he has been."

He looked upon the floor without speaking for awhile; then, as if he had made up his mind from a process of reasoning, said, "I think he best remain in prison over the Sabbath."

November 5, 1862.

Every turning of the glass brings out a new and ever more surprising combination of colors.

Today the whole house began to brighten. I say began, for it was only the opening of a cheerful aspect. Each day of the week past has added something to the hope or assurance that the old state of things was played out; Dr. Ottman was getting to feel the freedom of his own will, and *his* will is that of a gentleman and Christian. His will is always to make more comfortable everyone who comes into the house.

The closing of this day is not a part of the opening thereof; Dr. Clark, by some strange mistake of someone in power, is in the house again!

I do not know it until I am asked to go to the office. I start with alacrity to go, meet Dr. Ottman [and] say, "Do you wish to see me?" "No, Dr. Clark is in the office and asks for you!" My alacrity does not flag after this painful piece of information; I am not conscious of wrongdoing; and I have defended this man, as I have told you.

So I open the door—he is standing in the middle of the room, with his cap on, and does not lift it, but as I bow looks fiercely at me, and with a voice trembling with rage exclaims, "Mrs. Ropes, you will leave this house early tomorrow morning!"

There are some minds which excite antagonism in me at once, but this man never moves or hits me. And my answer was, accordingly, "Certainly sir, if it is for the good of the hospital and such is the 'order,' but I believe I am 'ordered' not to leave on any consideration."

"Who dares give 'orders' here but me?"

"My 'order' was from Secretary Stanton!"

You have seen a soldier erect and firm in the line of drill, when released, fold down some inches and wrinkle up generally. Well, so did Dr. Clark, as though one had "hit him beneath the thigh."

"His office is higher than mine, but we can't live here together."

"It *would* be unpleasant," I replied, and turned and left the room. Once in my own, where I had to play the part of hostess to a half starved cadet—and who, being a small man, astonished me with the amount of bread, butter, and tea he had consumed—I still found time to carry on another train of thought which ended in my going back to the office. The Doctor had seated himself close by his desk. I crossed his room to the fireplace. He was reading a document. In a very subdued tone he said, "Mrs. Ropes, I find Stanton's 'order' here awaiting me. You will please let *that all pass.*"

"Certainly, sir, but you spoke a moment ago as though I had done you some great wrong and I am not willing to let that pass, for I am not guilty."

He became excited again. I said, "Look at me, sir, and say how have I wronged you."

"I am master here. You should have no will above mine. What right had you to go down and look at that place where Julius was imprisoned?"

"I never did, sir. I do not know even in what part of the cellar it is."

He looked up sharply at me and exclaimed, "Then there have been dreadful lies told."

"Doubtless there have been, sir, but you will not question my word on a point of so little moment."

The conversation lasted some time longer, but was very unsatisfactory. I asked at length if there was anything more he wished of me and he answered no. I turned to go, saying, "It is a little strange that the only person in the house who has *defended you* should be also the only one whom you assail in this way." He did not reply by looking at me, but with his eyes on an open letter he said, "I only know that I have been in the Old Capitol Prison for nearly a week, and if you had not gone to Stanton it would not have been."

I thought over the facts for a moment and replied, "If the thing should happen again of one of the patients brought here to recover, and you allowed the steward to throw him into that place, I should run for help. Why? Because I am a mother, and I have only to remember that each of these sick ones [has] a mother somewhere, and for the time I act for them."

He seemed lost in thought. I said again, "Shall I go?"

"Certainly. Excuse my not offering you a seat."

"Oh, certainly! *Good breeding* is not the 'order' here." You may well believe I do not sleep much tonight, but God will not forsake my loss.

November 6, 1862.

The day drags heavily. I was up in the night to go my rounds; the half lit halls, the cold floors, and over all the sense of universal depression in the house made me feel as though I was all alone. I mounted to the third floor to look after some sick patients. One who I left, feeling as though he might not live through the night, I turned my steps to. He seemed as I left him. I took a chair by him, for the weary watcher had fallen asleep on the floor. Why should he not? He is but a convalescent patient, and instead of watching, why should he not be resting?[76] This lad is the only son of his mother and she a widow; he is unable to speak, and has been so from the time he came into the house. I go from him to others, and as the clock strikes four I go back to bed. Miss Low is in the same room with me.[77] I am glad though she is asleep, for it takes away the edge of my loneliness. When the day dawns one of my men has gone, and before the hour of supper time comes we close the eyes of two more, one the only son of his mother! The bright things of the night's summing up are that Miss Low has come again to sleep. And she brings me a message from the "Inspector." He says he ordered the release from the Capitol Prison of Dr. Clark solely on my plea for him! And if he continues to annoy the house, we have but to so state the case to him and he shall be returned again to the society of convicts.

But I shall make no efforts to hasten his discharge; the papers were put into the hands of the proper officer for his dismissal from service here, previous to his release. Strange that they are so long in coming. And strange too that [at] the moment of his appearance the gate is shut down upon supplies, and Miss Kendall is driven nearly frantic over the small amount of food for her ward. Today she said she did not know but she might have one more week of three meals each day, to be created out of *"nothing,"* but a longer time was not to be thought of.

76. Patients who had recovered sufficiently to be of assistance were often assigned nursing duties.

77. Low was apparently a transient nurse, awaiting assignment to another hospital.

The matter of food is bad enough, but I believe the depressing sphere of the house tells quite as much upon the men as anything else. Generally I have been able to bring a smile from the invalids, but now they curl their heads under the sheet and think it is of no use to try any longer to get well. I am glad this "Red Riding Hood" has come to stay all night. The "Armory" is in a state of repair, and she leaves to find a bed here.[78]

November 7, 1862.

We are surprised with a brisk snow storm and icicles hanging from the window sash. The snow is half a foot deep upon the shed roof, sloping from the cloth[es] room window. We must have forestalled New England. The house is very cold, the furnace not yet set, and no supply of coal on hand. I am burning dead oak wood in my room and indulge in a pair of socks and a bit of an old coverlet under my feet.

Army wagons are constantly passing, and my thoughts flit from them to the men in camps. Why could not this battle to be fought have come off while the roads were tolerable, and the sky clear and bright? The men who come in now come not with wounds, but with fevers.

An agent from the Sanitary Commission called to see what we are most in want of, and seemed ready to do anything we asked. I needed sugar, shirts, crackers, farina, drawers, and some chickens and oysters for the men who sit up but do not come down. He said he would come next Monday again. Much good has the "Sanitary" done for the soldiers. If they sometimes get "taken in," it is no more than all other organizations suffer from. Ah! Well! We must rest if we can and trust, for night closes in and the Doctor [A.M. Clark] is still here.

78. Louisa May Alcott considered the Armory Square Hospital excellent in comparison to Union Hospital. *Hospital Sketches,* 71.

November 8, 1862.

"Red-Riding-Hood" said good-bye for a permanency this morning after breakfast by my fire, said meal for two consisting of two pieces of corn cake and one piece of beefsteak. We [ate] from the same plate, having two little mugs for our tea, and [a] teapot as big as my fist. I miss the dear girl very much tonight, the time when she came tripping in with a smile.

But one can work at a better purpose in the Armory Hospital, whither she has gone. My view for myself is different. I can't leave this poor wretched place in its degradation; I must stand by the worst of its life, hoping for brighter things.

Dr. Clark is here. We feel him, as one does an east wind, or scent him, as a disagreeable odor. He goes no more into the wards; I fear the men would hiss at him if he did. Everybody seems out of humor; even the head cook has come to me to say he longed to knock the surgeon down, that the men come to him and complain for want of food, and how can I get it for them when there are no more rations in the house? Louis is a good humored German and excellent cook.[79]

I set Fanny [Warren] to making him a cup of tea while he tells me furthermore that he is *drunk;* that he was so unhappy about the fare, he had been deliberating and got drunk! He has no sooner drunk his tea and gone about his business, making a great noise in the court—meeting Dr. Clark and threatening to stick the bread knife into him, and laughing loudly when that courageous gentleman gives a leap of three stairs up into the open space by the court door—than Miss Kendall appears to tell me of her mission.

All the week I have been unwilling to leave the house for a moment; but I kept the remembrance of Dr. Perley's kind offer to help me always fresh in mind, as a reserved force if I became too close pushed—that strait appeared today.

79. This was Louis Herman, Cook, B Co., 39th Ill. Regiment, attached to Union Hospital on Aug. 8, 1862. MR-NA.

Some days ago Dr. Clark gave orders in the surgery that no article should be given to me either from that room or the store room any more than to one of the privates. It was an insult many in the house were ready to resent, but it did not affect me so; I felt strong in the fact that a petition from me to the Inspector would take him back to prison. But today he seemed to delight so in the exercise of brief power over others, and among them Dr. Ottman, countermanding his order for invalids' food and for a gridiron that Louis might cook steak easier, that I wrote a note to Dr. Perley and begged Miss Kendall to take it to him.

While she was absent the chaplain came in and relieved his mind.

"When shall we be rid of this tyranny? The boys are suffering with cold; I begin to think Brother Ottman and myself have been remiss in duty. We ought to have moved in this matter before, for this is a godless man, I am convinced, a godless man. Now here are two hundred people beside assistants made miserable through the power of this man. It must not be, indeed it must not!"

"Well, why don't you go enter a complaint?"

"I hate to do it. I hate to badger a fox when he is run into his hole, and though he talks at the table in his usual pompous style we know where he has been and who can place him there again." The chaplain fidgeted on his chair with a mind disturbed from its calm, scholarly thoughtfulness, and unable to find in the wisdom of the schools a precedent to act from. Indeed, I was looking at him with surprise that he had spoken so plainly and decidedly, because when he was questioned by the man of law, sent out by Stanton, he seemed like one who had left his thoughts in his study from which he had been summoned. And I had not forgotten my disappointment at the want of clearness in his testimony. I think through all this troubled water the men have been much less clear in the sense of right than the women have. Is it that they hate to give up one of their own club to the law? Certainly, if ever there was a case demanding prompt action, it was this. The chaplain placed his back to the fire, nervously twisting and searching the pockets of his dressing gown. Miss Kendall, restive to tell me of the success or failure of her mission (I could not tell which) rested the tip of her glove upon the table. The tableaux changed—he was gone and my brown eyed little friend had the chance she needed.

My note, which she gave to the servant, soon brought a request for her to walk into the parlor. Over the note the brow of the Inspector clouded, while half to her and half to himself he commented upon its contents: "I released this man at her earnest solicitations; he rewards her with impertinence. I wish I had listened to my own and the Secretary's better judgment and kept him where he richly deserves to be, in the Old Capitol Prison. If I order his arrest again I must eat my own words, for I have made out my report favorable to him purely on her testimony. What do *you* think?"

[Kendall:] "I think the only thing worth considering is the result now, and in the future of this war, on the good comfort of the soldiers. He is but one—he has done them constant and heart-sickening injustice, not only in the matter of food, but in his manner on the wards. Why should he be spared?"

"Sure enough, sure enough. I ought not to be *too proud* to say I have made a mistake. I'll go first to the Surgeon General—if he won't do the right thing, I know the Secretary will or, stop, I'll have him arrested at once if you say so."

"If you do, how long would he have to stay in prison?"

"Three months perhaps, before a trial could be had."

"Oh, well, neither she [Ropes] or myself are prepared to act so as to involve so great consequences." The Inspector twirled the note thoughtfully.

"She hardly expected me to show this to the Secretary?" he said, holding it up.

[Kendall:] "Let me read it, I ask, because she said as she handed it to me, if it were not sealed I would like you to read it, and perhaps I can decide that for you."

He gave it to her, and when she had read it her woman's

intuition decided quickly that it was not to be shown to anyone but him to whom it was addressed.

The Inspector arose to go and my friend, sure things were put in the right train, came home. Some mysterious missive must have followed very soon, for the manner of the Doctor [Clark] was that of one who felt a fearful looking forth of judgment. He no longer talked large of "promotion," of "transfer," of being "ordered to the front." He kept in his room, busily writing. Just at night he handed letters to Dr. Ottman, saying he had reason to expect another arrest, that he was no longer on duty here, and, if he was arrested, he would like him to give the letters to the Surgeon General.

Sunday brought no arrest, but after the evening closed in the Doctor [Clark] ordered the wardmaster to take him in the ambulance to Washington. While on the road, he evinced his usual want of discretion by telling how it happened that he was not arrested. As soon as the Surgeon General heard what the Inspector had to say, he filled out the release from duty and sent an order out with it, enclosed in a note telling him [Clark] of the possible arrest. As soon as the papers were out of his office the detective from the War Department entered the rooms, asking for Dr. Clark. The surgeon [Clark] very coolly replied that he was no longer on duty, and he could not say for a certainty where he was! Dr. Clark chuckled over this piece of intrigue as a very good joke.

As for the Surgeon General, a man who could not be more nobly loyal and true to the Secretary of War, [Clark] deserves little favor at his hands or the hands of his countrymen. For the past few days Dr. Clark has been riding a fast horse past the hospital, and on one occasion brought his wife into his old office here. I do not know if anyone saw them to speak to them outside of that room. My lips have been closed upon their haps and mishaps.

November 12, 1862.

I may as well confess that I like the patients very much better before they are able to be dressed and walk out.

Spitoons and tobacco cuds, not to say tobacco juice, mark the path of those who are considered worthy of "passes." And after the "passes" comes whiskey in its worst form, poisoned doubtless. Saturday is sure to end with a tendency to the guardhouse. If it be a hardened old soaker, one hands him over with only a moment's thought; but if it be one long sick, long petted, and anxiously watched, every loophole of escape from punishment is sought with a pity that will not be set aside unheard or unheeded.

The first point of interest which I nailed to the wall, as a trophy of the true mettle of the man, were the words of our new surgeon, on his first Saturday evening, when several men came in, wild with liquor.[80]

His office door opened silently upon their advancing steps—steadied by the guard—and more in sadness than anger he exclaimed, "Poor devils! Haven't they used you *bad* enough here, that you must go and treat yourselves *worse*? Wardmaster! Do your duty!" And with a side turn, as though he did not wish to condemn beyond recall, he swung himself back within the office.

George, the noisiest of these delinquents, is a pleasant New York volunteer with a badly wounded foot, difficult to save, broken open and bleeding afresh from the excitement and stumble of tonight.

The Wardmaster, himself a wounded inmate of the hospital, now recovered, but too recent not to remember the pain, is tender to this man, and instead of taking him into new and close quarters, smuggles him into the reading room, onto his own bed.[81] Close by that bed is a man lying, panting for breath from enlargement of the heart. I am fanning him,

80. R. Ottman, acting assistant surgeon, was in charge of Union Hospital from Saturday, Nov. 8, 1862, to Monday, Nov. 10, 1862. He was succeeded on Nov. 10 by George W. Stipp, surgeon, U.S. Volunteers, who was in charge until March 27, 1863. IMO-NA.

81. The wardmaster was Corp. Richard Trevor, F Co., 31st N.Y. Volunteers. Wounded on June 27, 1862, he was attached to Union Hospital on July 5, 1862. MR-NA.

but turn to hush George, who swears. He stops at once. A little whiskey makes a man truthful even to his own injury. Three weeks before, in distributing a delicacy to the patients of this room, one portion was stolen before I got round. Of course nobody did the act, so far as confession would bring the thing to light. I was indignant at the one man's loss and said I should not serve them again. I had forgotten the circumstance, but much extra suffering in other wards had really kept me away more than usual. George in his crazy fit told the whole story. He, the last one I should have suspected, had accepted a division of it, offered by a lubberly clown who was his near neighbor on the other side. He asked me to forgive him, held up his hand for me to take it as a token that I had, and "would call it square." In a room where so many sick men need quiet, one is at their wits' end to devise means of soothing. The deposits of his stomach were on the floor [on] either side of the narrow bed, and his throbbing temples [were] burning with fever. It was too late in the night for coffee. I gave him cider vinegar to drink; it turned the sickness. I said, "Now say your prayer, with closed eyes, and you will fall asleep."

[George:] "Well! I *used to* though, but it's a long while ago—couldn't remember all now; look here, will you help me through, if I begin?"

"Certainly." Twice he halted but was set quickly right; his spirit was receiving the repose, falling so divinely from a state higher than his own. The eyelids ceased to quiver, other lips spoke for him verses from the psalms and lines from familiar hymns—"beautiful," said the lad, a child[like] expression settling over his face. Sleep had gathered the helpless soul into her motherly, all-forgiving arms, and consciousness uttered no reproach till the sun of a new day lit the clear heavens with the soft mellow brightness of a rare November morning. When I went in to see him, it was with a cup of coffee in my hand and no allusion to the previous night in my looks or words. But in the course of the day he told me of the remorse and humiliation which oppressed him, and the overpowering sense of kindness he had received, ending with a solemn vow never to so dishonor his manhood again.

Alas for the poverty of true manliness, the great overmastery of human weaknesses! How often, with the puling infirmity of absolute imbecility, do these men excuse themselves—"I have such a habit"—as though the price of the greatest gift heaven ever proferred (human manhood) must be paid for less than the old patriarch's mess of pottage!

"A habit!"—that of chewing a vile cud no four footed animal would venture to roll under their tongue!—that of drinking vile liquor, too vulgar in odor to use even for a foot wash!

Ah, Man, my hitherto pride and admiration! My much loved brother, even while pity fills my eyes with tears, unspeakable shame tingles on my cheeks!

Duane is better. We have him up and dressed; the nurse says he is full of mischief now and is a trouble to the other patients. A happy Irish boy of seventeen, he is droll and jolly—so full of life one wonders how he could be so very sick with fever and rally so quickly. The men about him are in middle life, sober and tame—he is a prancing colt among them. What pranks he plays upon them—stealing the bread from one, a comb from another, and yesterday an apple from a man who had, in simple faith of its security, entrusted a nice large apple upon the hearth to roast. Naughty Duane had eaten it up without compunction! More from audacious mischief than malice aforethought! The owner of the apple looked like one suffering a great wrong with Christian patience and dogged silence. Not so the nurse. She would have removed him from the room for his "ugliness."

Just now I took some baked apples into the room for a very sick patient. Duane sat by the fire, noisy with talk and singing. I hushed him. "Oh maam, it is the good apples ye are giving to Baily I am often fretting for."

"Ah, and which commandment are you breaking by so doing?"

"Thou shalt not covet!"

"And which one was it you broke yesterday when you took the apple from the fire?"

"Thou shalt not steal!"

"So you do know the commandments. Please repeat them all." He commenced, and went through the ten commands without losing a word or any apparent sense of having ever broken one of them, unless in a somewhat heightened color in his cheeks.

Turning to go out I noticed Powers, a man from New Hampshire whose bed is near the door, and asked if the noise troubled him. He said, "Very much." I stooped over him—he seemed a good deal sick, and I ordered his bed moved into a more quiet place. He suddenly lifted his hand and caught mine, exclaiming with more emotion than I ever knew him to show before, "Thank you. Nobody seems to think I am very sick."[82] This man has a truly beautiful character. He came in from Harper's Ferry with several others, one a little boy of thirteen, waiter to the Colonel of the regiment. This boy we consider a blessing in the house. He told me Mr. Powers was so kind. "He took me in his arms when his knapsack was on his back and he staggered most all the way, he was so weak—for he was sick too, but he said he would not leave me behind."

"How far did he carry you?"

"Way down to the Depot, much as a quarter of a mile."

Mr. Powers is endowed with new beauty to my mind since I heard that, though I had noticed his unselfish care of the motherless boy from the day they came.

• The hectic pace of Ropes's daily activities brought on a severe attack of neuralgia in mid-November. With a history of rheumatism and the strenuous demands of her present hospital life, complicated by her conflict with the steward and head surgeon, she

82. This was Pvt. Joshua Powers, F Co., 10th N.H. Volunteers. Powers was admitted to Union Hospital on Oct. 29, 1862, and died on Nov. 21, 1862. MR-NA.

now suffered "such torture as one cannot well smile on gra-
ciously."[83]

November 20, 1862.

. . . For three days the "matron" {Ropes] has been hived
within these four walls of dirty paper and shattered windows,
doing battle with this invisible monster, playing bo-peep up
her back, over her shoulders, into her left ear (there she was
valiant, for are not all her family vulnerable in that echoing
tube?) and she followed its entrance with a barricade of
chloroform and aconite; with a sharp slap on the temples,
escape was gained! I think she behaved very courageously till
the mean imp of evil stabbed her in both eyes! Then she sat in
dark silence for about twelve hours. At length its grasp
loosened, and wasn't she tired! . . .

Such queer things as women are! Mrs. Hopkins has hung
around two of her dying men till they were deluded into the
idea that she was justly entitled to all their earthly
possessions. Of course the homely instincts of the venerable
matron were antagonistic to any such arrangement, and she
adroitly dished those expectations by making a transfer of
them to the heirs at law.[84]

No sooner is the house settled and aired, after this influx
from the lower regions of selfishness, than Cashman and
Daremus have a *set-too,* a war of words.[85] They so berate each
other with rough, unshod, and ungloved expressions that
your matronly friend almost repented calling them into her
room, hoping to make an amicable settlement of the
blistering words they had thrown at each other through
mischief-loving go betweens. And though she can lift a
sledge hammer to defend the right, with a spasmodic courage

83. HAR to EPC, May 19, 1856; Ropes diary, excerpted portion, entry of
Nov. 20, 1862, SRC-UCR.
84. This was Edith A. Hopkins, a volunteer nurse. MR-NA.
85. Ropes refers to nurses Sarah J. Cashman and Julia Daremus.
MR-NA.

that is frightful to herself, when it is all over and she looks back this rattle of small arms, this vile odor of sulphurous breaths, silences her into a smothered pain whereof no word measure can be taken. I think all she said was, "Are you two women Christians?" The question was unexpected, and when the answer came it was in softened voices and simultaneous, "No, I don't think I am!"

"I am very glad to hear you say so," was the sad reply. A few hours took one of the belligerents on an indefinite furlough, the significance of which you can comprehend, and an order from the new surgeon placed the other high and dry upon the third floor, where her executive powers will have free chance to ultimate and the truer qualities of her mind blossom into a beautiful womanhood.[86]

Our pretty widow, young and buxom, will probably take charge of the sick diet.[87] My other protégée reminds me of the truly medicinal and valuable burdock in autumn. No one can touch even the outer verge of its richly rooted broad leaves without being covered with *burrs*. I could wish, while I love her very much, that someone less nervous, more healthy minded, and more genial to the other nurses filled her place. But while I write my heart enters a *protest*—she has won her niche there, and such hold their own. The faults or peculiarities one has taken by the hand are easier to hold than new ones may prove—let us bide as we are! There's consistency for you!

There is a great stir in the army and a constant din of passing. I do not mind it as much, now the windows are down and up (those in this hospital can alone understand *that*). . . .

November 21, 1862.
The nurse came and asked me to go in and see Powers; he lay sleeping quietly, under cover of which the angels were

86. The new head surgeon was George W. Stipp.
87. This was probably Edith A. Hopkins. See entry of Dec. 8, 1862, below.

loosing him from the clay prison, the hospital life so painfully distasteful to him, and making ready for him a home for which he pined in silence, for which he was so eminently fitted. I was glad he was unconscious, for he had a wife and two pretty children; their likeness lay under the pillow where his head rested, with the death damp dripping like tears onto the case so precious to him! Above his head was his Bible, presented by his wife, with her name on the flyleaf. Everything about him betokened respectability of soul and life.

The little boy drew his character truly. He sits here in my room, swallowing down the tears of real bereavement for his friend. What for has the man saved the child?

November 24, 1862.

Thanksgiving close upon us! Plenty of patients from states wherein Thanksgiving Day is *the* holiday of the year! What is to be done? The good Doctor says we must make the men happy on that day! As though that were possible with a ration of bread and meat! No turkeys and no pies!

Is not man an animal, specially appreciative of the difference between hay and clover? And what can render that sensitiveness of stomach, which makes him in fact merely a stomach, more alive than the starvation of war, culminating in fever from which he is convalescent?

Pies cannot be cooked in a hospital—that is, a young hospital like this, a hospital which at any age of respectable maturity would still be a one-horse establishment.

Ah! There are some advantages in being a humble creature of "Sanitary" charity. The "matron" will beg pies! Yes! and add with an ill used look, "Anything else will be very acceptable." She will nip the burrs all out from her goodly Dock and send her along the streets of this would-be city, begging fodder for her boys![88] Our Dock has great executive

88. "Dock" was either Sarah J. Cashman or Julia Daremus. See entry of Nov. 20, 1862, above.

power—it certainly could not fail her here because she is really interested in the success of the work.

The night closes in auspiciously. "Dock" has made a "raid" upon the oyster shops along the street, who in our individual pocket we have much patronized, and they promise her well. We will trust to her rare perseverance the redemption of those promises.

The "matron" has located her field of labor upon the [Georgetown] "heights." The beautiful "Heights!" from which the ripened browns of the closing year are visible, . . . Among the falling leaves, too, are seen the white tents nestling under the oaks for shelter, or stiffly resisting the winds on the summit of still higher "heights" towards the west.[89]

To the south, the rough part of the town. Shops and shop people are out of sight in the valley below the bluff—only chimneys tell of settlement. Beyond them stretches the now historic Potomac—calm, of uncertain color and clearness, but broad, secure in its power and protection from the tufted steep wall of Virginia, gleaming at night with camp fires, by day dotted everywhere with tents. Gazing from this far point of so much home beauty, one watches with eager interest the steep footpaths, worn into the sandy slopes, and loves to gaze at the faithful men who every hour for many a long month have kept between us and our foes!

At your feet, even today, delicate flowers bloom! Through the paling of the cemetery fence, eyes of purple, white, pink, and yellow cheer and brighten the somber shade of the sturdy oaks and cluster among the vines almost to the eaves of the chapel, the sides of which are covered with English Ivy! God smiles always! His benediction now, when war strides over the land! What can be said of the gentle eyes of women who greet me along the "heights"—*loyal* and *true* ladies!—where loyalty costs a world of feeling and a mine of wealth!

---

89. Ropes went to Georgetown Heights to ask Mrs. M.M. Boyce for help in preparing the Thanksgiving celebration.

There is never a day of summer heat so weary and
discouraging that some token of goodwill or pleasant
greeting was not sure and waiting for me! Now also, the want
of the soldier is anticipated. The venerable matron goes back
rich in the promises that never fail.

• The troubles with hospital administrators finished and her illness gone, Ropes turned her enthusiastic attention to preparations
for the Thanksgiving celebration. Her concern for the patients
showed not only in her official actions, but in personal attentions
toward the men and a determination not to return home for
Thanksgiving should she be able to make that holiday more pleasant for them. Accordingly she wrote home to Alice, informing her
of that fact.

November, 1862 [No Date]
My dear little girl,
However much I may desire to go and see you all on
Thanksgiving Day it is out of the question. I can't leave "my
boys." More than you imagine they need me, at all hours. If
they are getting better the star of their hope is to be able to
walk into my room, a mysterious place of comfort from
which springs all their little luxuries and [regarding] which I
amuse them by telling about what part of the building it is in,
how many steps they will have to go down to reach it, and
[that] they shall have two spoonsful of wine in a little tumbler
and a Boston cracker if they will be good and try to get well.
That last you will think strange of. Yet it is even so. The poor
fellows are weary of life; a week ago one sent for me to come
to him, the nurse telling me he could not live till night. I
talked with him awhile, and found he had made up his mind
to die. I told him he had no right to any mind about it, no man
could know the bounds of his life, and he must consider his,
worn and emaciated as it was, the gift of God, for him to use
as long as the gift was placed at his command. I came down
and sent up a half tumbler of [the hospital's] best port wine by
the needle woman, telling her to give it *all* to him. He said,

never [had] anything tasted so good as that. In two hours I sent up a cup of arrowroot seasoned with wine; that, with Mrs. Warren's declaration to him that she should dance at his wedding, brought almost a smile upon his lips. Last night I went again to see him. He certainly is better. Who knows but this Virginian may live to tell of the war to his grandchildren?

Mrs. Boyce calls on Sunday with her carriage and takes me home to dine with her—that is my only pastime and it is great.

She is to help me about pies for Thanksgiving, for the whole house, 250 people! Give my love to Grandma, Mrs. Sumner, and Mrs. Barnard *particularly,* and everybody else. *Keep all my letters,* gather them up everywhere you can. We live so much that I forget, and my discussions in letters are always the most graphic. Keep the ms. *carefully* . . . .

Your mother
H.A.R.

• The Thanksgiving celebration to which Ropes looked eagerly forward was successful, and her efforts in behalf of the hospital must have been highly appreciated by the patients. She recorded the event in her diary.

November 27, 1862.

A day always to be remembered! How kind people are everywhere! The oyster dealers have been so liberal that every man has had his bowl of oyster soup. The best thing to me was that our secret was kept from the patients. Early in the morning our pretty widow, with one of the attendants, started for the "heights" to get flowers and vines for the dining room. Meanwhile, the "matron" [Ropes] was receiving loads of that time honored concomitant of Puritan Thanksgiving—designated, in the aggregate, *pies*—in detail, apple, mince, peach, and pumpkin. The last mentioned [is] not a native subject of this District, and in this instance the lady [M.M. Boyce] assured me that after giving explicit directions to her contraband cook, fresh from the Fredericksburg exodus, she only saved the pies from an "upper crust" by an anxious suspicion which led her in timely season into her cook room!⁹⁰

The matron, feeling anxious as elderly people are apt to, withdrew to the subterranean dining room, where one soldier sat as guard over numberless piles of plates and bowls; she wisely takes him into her counsels and thus secures a valiant ally. The pretty widow, rosy with the morning air and eyes sparkling with the autumn beauty upon which they have just gazed, appears with the tall, manly [attendant], bearing his basket filled with flowers and overhung almost to the floor with trailing periwinkle, fresh as in June, and rich, sober green vines of English Ivy. Ah! Don't you envy us our treasures, you who hover over big fires and tread on soft carpets, who echo a glum sound from the frozen gravel over which you tread to the Thanksgiving service? These live tokens of nature's generosity to my sweet and gentle friend on the "heights" [M.M. Boyce], who ever gives as freely as she has received, make even the "matron" feel young again. She is truly good humored today, if not thankful. Nay, her homely face lights up from under the deep lines with the words oftenest on her lips, when bending over the sick and dying, "Bless the Lord, Oh my Soul, who crowneth thee with loving kindness and tender mercy."⁹¹

• Thanksgiving over, Ropes's thoughts returned to routine hospital affairs and her recent bout with the steward and head surgeon. Writing to a friend, she described the affair in condensed form. Her adventures, she suspected, might be interesting—and saleable—to the public, and she made preliminary preparations for possible

90. Washington, D.C., was filled with contraband slaves. By Nov. 1862, around 3,000, primarily from Virginia, South Carolina, and Georgia, had established a camp near the city. Livermore, *My Story of the War,* 257.

91. Notation on reverse side of Nov. 27 entry: "This is wholly unfinished."

publication. Her Kansas experience had produced a book, and she apparently had every intention of making her hospital activities likewise known.

Union Hospital
Georgetown, D.C.
December 8, 1862

My Dear kind friend,[92]

. . . This hospital has had an exciting history since you left. No one remains here of the surgeons whom you knew, and only two of the patients—Louis, in the kitchen, and Trevor, who was in the reading room with a wound in the leg, and who is now a most excellent wardmaster.[93]

Of the nurses, Miss Stevenson stayed till October, then went to Boston to rest. Miss Kendall has just returned from a visit home. Mrs. Hopkins has charge of invalid diet, with a nice cooking stove in the small kitchen of the small house. Miss Best has the ward on the second floor front.[94] The others are strangers and mere hired nurses, disposed as nurses seem disposed to be from time immemorial.

We had a terribly sick house through September and October. Twelve men with amputated limbs, and other dreadful wounds. Dr. Ottman came as assistant, a very fine gentleman from Pennsylvania, and Dr. Hinkle, from Philadelphia, came in to help us through the worst of the first two weeks. Dr. Clark was put in charge. He was a man of small powers, a great idea of the dignity inherent in *straps*—talked large. The new steward who came in was a Frenchman, without principle, and rather large brain. Such a state of things as two months brought about you can hardly conceive. The men were starved, the clothes were stolen, the

92. Possibly Dr. William Hays, who had served earlier with Ropes at Union Hospital.

93. Ropes refers to Louis Herman and Richard Trevor. Alcott disapproved of the use of convalescents as attendants instead of healthy, properly trained men. *Hospital Sketches,* 74.

94. Margaret Best was a volunteer nurse. MR-NA.

rations were sold. It [culminated] in the thrusting of one of the boys into a dark hole in the cellar. As you may believe, it did not take me long to go in to Washington to Stanton, who very promptly arrested the steward and sent him to the Old Capitol [Prison]. The day following, Dr. Clark was also arrested and placed in limbo at the same quarters! Stanton behaved splendidly. The prompt action startled all the doctors and the stewards in the District. Dr. [Clemens?] tried to have me removed. Stanton said it should not be done, and ordered him to go to the "front." We now are having peaceable times with Dr. Stipp for head surgeon. The men have enough to eat; the clothes are washed in the back room of the small house, where a huge boiler is set.

Winter, 1862
[No Date]

My Dear Alice,

. . . I send by the same mail two large envelopes containing leaves cut out of my journal. Let anybody read them who likes, but don't lose them. I had thought if the [Boston] "Advertiser" would send me a *good price* for them to print without the names, your uncle may sell it, but if so I will want a few copies sent to me. Perhaps the "Atlantic" would buy it.[95]

I decided to send the large packages to your uncle Peleg. You can have them after he has read them.

You have no idea how much relieved I am to feel that you are with such kind people for the winter. God forever bless them for the favor shown you. And *I* am sure you will be agreeable to them.

We have our steward in a *safe place,* on bread and water. Miss Boyce has just called with Mrs. Dr. Hinkle. The Doctor is better, and there is hope of his recovery—he is a model surgeon, we think.

95. In similar fashion, Katharine Prescott Wormeley admonished her mother to save her wartime letters. *The Other Side of the War,* 125, 137–38.

So confused is the house that the wardmaster has not been able to send yet for the boxes. . . .

My room is comfortable and everyone is kind to me.[96] The winter will soon be over, and I shall not think of staying through another hot season. I send Ned's last letter. Write to him even if you do not hear.

Miss Stevenson's box has arrived today. Thank Aunt Eliza for the hood—I need it very much in the entries, they are so cold—also for the scarf and bottles. I have given out Miss Stevenson's things for her boys. They are her most devoted admirers and accepted their presents with bright eyes and quivering lips. Write often as you can. My best love to the family of Barnards.

Your loving Mother
H.A.R.

Winter, 1862
[No Date]

My Dear Little Girl,

A short letter will be better than none to you, and that is all I can do for you. I have to answer many letters *for* the men, and *to* them after they leave.

I don't seem to need any clothes, . . . perhaps some stockings may be wanted before spring, white cotton. I sent some boots and shoes back . . . to be changed for a size smaller. What became of them? No need of laying out money for me, child. If anybody sends me voluntary presents, of course, they are very pleasant to receive.

You spoke of Mrs. Ware, saying they would send a box. Of course we shall be very glad to receive one.

Our most pressing wants are shirts, drawers, and stockings for winter wear. Also plain, unbleached, rather small sized cotton shirts. I do not think so much of jellies and preserves as of wine, brandy, tea, and coffee. Also, butter crackers.

96. According to Alcott, the nurses' quarters were not at all comfortable. *Hospital Sketches,* 50, 67.

Mr. Barnard's last summer's gift of tea and crackers and old brandy lasted like the "widow's cruse," and did untold good. I don't think I could have stood the summer without that nourishing breakfast tea. It was meat and drink to Miss Stevenson and myself. And the patients have begged me for my "likeness" with the cup in my left hand, and my dressing gown on, a candle in my right hand; this is my "rig" in the night when I go over the wards to see how the sickest are. . . . spring will soon be here, and *peace* I hope. Dr. Stearns came as a great surprise last Saturday. What a fine fellow he is![97]

Ned has sent me a nice letter. Did you send him the gloves? Thank Aunt Eliza for the firkin. The shirt is on my precious self, also a pair of the drawers. I wear socks all the time over my shoes. Tell her the apple butter was served round to Pennsylvania Germans, whose eyes sparkled over it.

. . . Shall send some more journal as soon as I get time to pick it up together. Write often. I rode down to look at the Senate. They appear in better trim than when they went home—clean suits of clothes, well cut hair, &c. &c. Special love to Barnards, in great haste—[98]

• December 1862 was a grim month for Union military fortunes. Major General Ambrose E. Burnside, having succeeded McClellan, proceeded to demonstrate his incapacity for supreme command. Missing opportunities to strike isolated rebel forces, he hurled his 114,000 men against a united, well-entrenched Confederate army of 72,000 at Fredericksburg, Virginia, on December 13. Although the rebels were ensconced behind virtually impregnable positions, Burnside ordered repeated attacks which the Southern defenders dispelled with tremendous destructiveness. Direct assault tactics, suicidal in view of the opponents' defenses, resulted in almost 13,000 Federal casualties, compared to little more than 5,000 for the Confederates. The disaster at Fredericksburg

97. Stearns, not recorded on the hospital muster rolls, was possibly a civilian volunteer.
98. The 3rd session of the 37th Congress opened on Dec. 1, 1862.

brought Union hopes to an unprecedented low. Lincoln drew bitter political fire, talk of peace negotiations with the South increased, and faith in the national future began among many to waver.

Visible reminders of the battle streamed back into Washington, a "distressful spectacle" of torn, defeated warriors, weakened by wounds, illness, and exposure, transported in rough conveyances or shuffling and limping in doleful procession to obtain the medical aid they so badly needed. A major portion had suffered wounds in the upper parts of the body as a result of being shot while trying to take the elevated rebel positions. To the hospitals they came, the hospitals which at such times were never empty, and of whose personnel extraordinary exertion was required. Transportation for the wounded was so inadequate that the last patients were not received in the Washington hospitals until the end of December.[99] Amid the despair and frantic effort to care for the victims of Fredericksburg, Hannah Ropes remained uninfluenced by defeatism. Her account of the situation began with her diary entry of December 13, 1862.

December 13, 1862.

A glorious atmosphere, soft winds drift through the bare boughs of the trees noiselessly. Everybody and everything seems listening, in smothered silence. Transports are leaving the shore of the Potomac, close in front of the hospital, for Aquia Creek; five of our attendants were ordered on board of one two days since; and this evening our kind and skillful surgeon, Dr. Ottman, has been sent to the "front." The matron has drummed together the steward with a candle in one hand and a plate of cold pork in the other, [and] the pretty widow, with a loaf of bread and butter. Trevor has cut the bread before the cloth[es] room fire. She [Ropes] has spread it, and between them a big bundle of sandwiches have been made and packed in a valise, with plenty of towels and a flask of old brandy, six apples, and a piece of old castile soap. What a beautifier an earnest and benevolent purpose is! How handsome the Doctor looked! Even his wife, sad as it must

99. Brooks, *Washington, D.C., in Lincoln's Time,* 16, 47.

have made her, was glad to have him go. We are cheered by the arrival of Miss Alcott from Concord—the prospect of a really good nurse, a gentlewoman who can do more than merely keep the patients from falling out of bed, as some of them seem to consider the whole duty of a nurse.[100]

All the week we have been getting ready for the expected battle,[101] yet every day our beds are full of sick from camps—even though each morning finds us sending off some farther north. This has been our mode of action ever since the hospital opened, a way station for those who need to come and be made comfortable till ordered farther north.

December [14?], 1862.

This is Sabbath morning in good Old New England; here, in this semi-civilized District, the drum beats; soldiers are marching, some east to Washington, some west to the bridge spanning the Potomac and connecting us with Old Virginia.

There is generally a noise, mingled sound of active purposes, and wailing griefs. Still, the bright southern sun lies lovingly across my table onto the paper where my thoughts drip from the pen. Let it be to you for whom I write a benediction.

The old face bending over it is doubly furrowed now, filled with deep lines. How many eyes she has closed! and, for the sake of, in sorrowing memory of their friends at home, laid a kiss upon their serene brows so cold, but peaceful! aye! restful!

Often, when the old mother face turns to go away from one dying bed to another, the breaking voice has whispered, "Don't go! It is so good to see a smile somewheres!" As though she did not carry the whole army in her pouch, and

100. This was Louisa May Alcott, of Massachusetts, author of *Hospital Sketches* and subsequent popular works. Alcott served as a volunteer nurse in Union Hospital until stricken with typhoid pneumonia in Jan. 1863. Her service there covered only about six weeks.
101. Ropes refers to the Battle of Fredericksburg.

bear crucifixion for her country! But to these she turns the side whereon the smile of God always shines, and, flinging all theology to the bats and owls, whispers with cheerfulness, "Who should you fear? The angels are here; God is the Friend who never forgets us, you will never be hungry or tired anymore," and she believes it as she says it!

This is God's war, in spite of uncertain generals, in spite of ill success; in spite of our own unworthiness; the cause is that of the human race, and must prevail. Let us work then with a good heart, here and at home. We are all scholars in the same school. Having failed to learn in prosperity, we ought to be glad of the Divine Mercy which gives us another chance in the upheaving of all social comforts and necessities.

Now is the judgment of this world. Each man and woman is taking his or her measure. As it is taken even so must it stand—it will be recorded. The activities of war quicken into life every evil propensity as well as every good principle.

No soul now can stand on neutral ground. Between truth and error there surges and foams a great gulf, but a *respectably* dressed crowd line the shore of dishonesty! Let *us* be *loyal* and *true,* then if the great world never hears a word about us one shall not fear, even though the waves of war's uncertain tide swallow us in the general wreck!

As usual, I have jumped away from the detail of hospital life in writing—facts, perhaps, in the hospital would give a different verdict, so believe for me all the good you can, giving me the benefit of every doubt.

December 17, 1862.

Seventy one men have come today. None very badly wounded, or rather but few of them, and in two days forty of them were forwarded to Philadelphia.

• The next few days were consumed with handling wounded soldiers from the Fredericksburg battlefield. Ropes continued her description of events in letters to Alice and to a friend, possibly Dr.

William W. Hays, with whom she had previously worked at Union Hospital.

> Union Hospital
> [No Date: Probably
> December 21, 1862]

Dear Alice,

This has been too busy a week for me to write at all. On Monday we packed off 38 men to other hospitals, and Tuesday received 71. After getting them nicely cared for, the "order" came for us to send 40, the least wounded, further north. Yesterday (Saturday) that unpleasant job was done, for they were loth to go, and it left us with a house full of dirty clothes in place of clean ones worn away. Today we are waiting for a fresh supply of worse wounded from the Fredericksburg battles, or murder ground I might say.

I dare say it looks worse to you in Boston than to us here. Burnside, nobody blames.[102] The President buries his heart in the middle states—he is honest, and that is some gain over anything we have had for President in some time. If Frémont had been left alone in Missouri, and Sigel in the Virginia mountains, we should not be as we are now.[103] This is a secession town, and you may be sure *they know* and rejoice over the blunder we made, and our tender regard for the institution of slavery. If in the beginning our President had declared freedom for all, and armed all, the rebellion would not have lasted three months. But the North was not ready to respond to such a scheme and here we are!

The true question was, whether we would have our sons sacrificed, or the blacks, for whose freedom this war is waged. We decided, as we always have done, pig-headedly—and

---

102. Maj. Gen. Ambrose E. Burnside commanded the Union forces at the Battle of Fredericksburg. Alcott referred to this battle as "the Burnside blunder." *Hospital Sketches,* 35.
103. Maj. Gen. John C. Frémont and Maj. Gen. Franz Sigel.

now the only way out of this trouble remains just where it did before, only to be gained by *immediate, unreserved emancipation.*

Declare for it, oh men of Boston! Forget all the lines of party—look at this thing from the standpoint of fifty years ahead, when the fever of political strife, with those who struggled for supremacy, has passed and gone.

The blacks are able and ready to free themselves; they only wait for legitimate "orders" to do it. Our chaplain is a Virginian, from its south line, a remarkable scholar, and a driven refugee from his home. He assured me that there is no telegraph so quick to communicate as the black race from one end of the country to the other.[104]

But I must not *preach* now, for my *use* is *work.* Dr. Perley sent for me last Sabbath, to dine at his house. I had a pleasant visit. Mrs. Fessenden and Mrs. Anderson were there. I am expecting Major Ladd today to take me into Washington to dine with him at the Wilsons'. I like Mrs. Wilson very much.

I should not have indulged in so large a sheet of paper, but the last influx of seventy one has swallowed up all small paper to inform anxious friends.

Major Ladd says he should like you to come on here with his wife in January, at his expense. But I have not encouraged it because I don't feel as though he was under any obligation for my care of him when he was sick, and also because I think you are doing more good where you are, and are much safer where you are.

The time has not come for you to go away from the only safe country in the world yet. I do not forget the possibility of our being together in this country, yet see no way at *present.* You have no idea of a hospital, nor has anyone who simply calls in to see me. We get *lousy!* and dirty. We run the gauntlet of disease from the disgusting *itch* to smallpox! My needle

104. Alcott had little respect for the chaplain, and was "afraid he still hankered after the hominy pots of Rebeldom." *Hospital Sketches,* 87.

woman found nine body lice inside of her flannel waistcoat after mending the clothes that had been washed! And I caught two inside the binding of my drawers!

I don't know of any price that would induce me to have you here!

Every patient, as soon as he is able, is cheered by the promise of coming to sit in my room. Sometimes one takes suddenly worse. I pick him up and lay him on the bed Miss Stevenson used to occupy, so as to give him extra care. You see, I have given myself to this work, not as the strutting officers on the avenue have, for a salary, and laziness, but for love of country. This sentiment sprang into active life in Kansas; it lives anew in this out of all rule district, where a high toned life is unknown.[105]

Where the strength comes from to do what I do is a mystery. I have had less neuralgia than usual and am perfectly free from it now. Don't worry about me. I shall send mighty quick of I am really sick, but . . . I shall go through the winter nicely. . . .

Only think! The old steward came from the prison to ask *my forgiveness* and the pardon of the house generally! The wardmaster was so sure that he would *dirk* me that he stood close between us, with his black eyes glowing like those of a lamb, ready to throttle him if he touched me. But no! He said he wanted my pardon. I held out my hand and said, "I owe no man anything but love. Take the lesson you have learned and go in peace."[106]

December 26, 1862
So much I wrote some time ago. Now I will try to get this into the mail though I hardly know how to direct to you, having never heard from you. The last battle of Fredericksburg has filled the house full of amputated limbs

105. Ropes's dedication to her patients was noted by Alcott. Ibid., 44–45.
106. Note on edge of letter: "My journal is very incomplete for want of time—and the constant interruption night and day."

again and we are full of care and work. Of course you see the papers, and know all that goes on and a great deal that has no foundation in fact.

We are not going to smash up generally as a nation. We have reached the last quarter of the night preceding the dawn. And, as in nature, [though] that hour is the most cheerless it is not less hopeless because of the approach of the new day. The government was never stronger than today, the people never more resolute. Money and supplies flow in from the North in a constant stream. But it is not of all this that I believe in success. No. The cause is not of either North or South—it is the cause of, and the special work of the nineteenth century, to take the race up into broader vantage ground and on to broader freedom. Without being at all an altruist I cannot fail to see the signs of the times. Now is the judgment of this generation. How plainly every man is being tested to show the true quality of his life, if he be a true man, honest, loyal, and noble as a countryman, or no. . . .

• Ropes's faith in human progress was reflected in her regard for the patients she treated. Appropriately enough, her final diary entry was concerned with the dignity and suffering of her charges.

December 27, 1862.

"Thank you, madam, I think I must be marching on." So said Lewie as he passed away. Sitting on one side of him was his nurse, Miss Alcott, on the other the matron [Ropes]. The remark was made to the latter, as she gave him a swallow of water. For ten days they have anxiously looked and longed and lingered over the possible facts in his favor. Three wounds under the shoulders, one bullet at least in the lungs or their vicinity—how could they hope for his recovery?

But there was in the man such a calm consciousness of life, such repose on its secure strength. There he lay, his broad chest heaving with obstinate breath, but the face as composed in its manly beauty, as though he were taking natural rest in sleep. The dignity of the man, considering the circumstances, was wonderful. In a room with a dozen others, a stony sort of room, close into the street, without one pleasant, attractive quality—it seemed as if he, in his individual force of purpose, must have revolted. But no, he did not—he was content to wait. And yet I do not think he was unconscious of the people thrown down about him from the same battlefield, or the disorder of the room. Feeling this, the matron took every care of his own bed, for he was a man, having his own views, a brave soldier who took up arms, having evidently counted the cost. And here he lies. Eight o'clock in the evening, the gas burning brightly. A man with one arm lying tenderly watching him on one side, and one with a fearful wound through the thighs on the other, who at last turns his face away, covering it with his blanket. Two hours before, Lewie had reached his right hand into Miss Alcott's lap and firmly grasped her wrist. He could not talk but a word at a time. The matron is left alone when the breath ceases—she, still watching with loving sympathy and a farther reaching consciousness of this process through which he is passing, keeps close by with her hand on his forehead, as though she would cross palms with the angels commissioned to take her work out of her hands.

The hair is at length smoothed, a lock cut from it to go to his mother, and the limbs straightened. The wondrous manly beauty of the whole person so impresses her that she sends the attendant to call Miss Alcott back. Even the attendant forgets the superstition of the early training he received, on the far source of the Kennebec, and admires God's work in this now deserted tenement. The matron, with fingers busy, says, "Frank, you are honored as never before by working hand to hand with those who receive this man, to do for him what you and I cannot." The good of the other patients demands that he be removed from the room and the matron, kissing him and saying, "Good by," turns to the other men to prevent if possible the ill effects of a false view of the orderly fact just past. Thus two of the last wounded closed their lives within the hospital, one a few hours after being brought in, the other this evening, after ten days sojourn with us.[107]

Two hands, small, thin and white, tremulous, reaching after things invisible, have laid in mine hour after hour today; two eyes like live coals roll, gleam, recede in terror behind their own pupils, or soften to tears before mine; two cheeks, purple with fever, a sweet mouth and beardless chin, teeth a girl might envy, and a wide fair brow, from which light brown hair, dank and curlless, falls away—this is the picture graved into the heart, fused with anxious pity! A face one hates to leave, knowing the physical danger of the lithe young creature whose crown it is.

But rest must be taken, and if I take another peep at him I will sleep. 5 o'clock in the morning: My boy has not closed his eyes, but tried all night to get away! to go to his camp, to answer the roll call, startled, frightened at the possible consequences of his non-appearance at his quarters. Too much brain, too little physical power; his ward physician is in his cups all day! and no attention given to this case! The most important ward in the hospital and the guiding spirit walking about among the amputated limbs like a somnambulist![108]

I wait till his round is over, and then call in the best of Christian gentlemen, Dr. Ottman. He pronounces him *very sick* and orders an anodyne—still, no closing, hardly to wink, of these bright, restless, beautiful blue eyes.[109]

• Thus ended Ropes's hospital journal. Soon she, too, would

---

107. Alcott recorded that patients, upon dying, "were carried away, with as little ceremony as on a battlefield." Such events, she said, were "bare of anything like reverence, sorrow, [or] pious consolation." *Hospital Sketches,* 86.

108. Drinking among surgeons was frequent. See Woolsey, *Hospital Days,* 27.

109. Alcott says that Ottman refused a better assignment at an officers' hospital in order "that he might serve the poor fellows at Hurlyburly House." *Hospital Sketches,* 99.

become a patient in Union Hospital. Her last three letters, written to a former patient, Edward, and Alice, describe her final nursing activities and the onset of what would prove to be a fatal case of typhoid pneumonia.

ɚ

>Union Hospital
>Georgetown, D. C.
>December 29, 1862

My Dear boy,

I was very glad to hear of your safe arrival home, for it seemed a long while since you left the hospital.

Your roommates have nearly all changed since you left. Only Frocin and Lee remain. The former will be sent to St. Elizabeth's Hospital for the fitting [of] his leg.

Since the last battle, the house is full of very bad cases; some 20 amputated limbs, to say nothing of other wounds. Your room has two with one leg, and one with only a right arm. Upstairs one man has only a part of one hand left, and that is now useless from the wound. So you will understand that we have our hearts and hands full. We have one Rebel in the ballroom with an amputated leg, and we take just as good care of him as of anyone.[110] Everything goes on nicely. The Christmas celebration was a great success, and the men had plenty of poultry and oysters. The weather is as warm as June and the air cheering. I am glad to know you're among friends; and you must not feel at all as though you shall not get entirely well. I never expected that you could go back to the camp. Army life demands just what you have lost, ability to travel. But you are young; recuperative power is inherent in the young, and you may be even a stronger man for the idle life you are obliged to live just now. Years from now, you will be surprised to look back and feel how full the items of today filled your thoughts and clouded your hopes. Believe me, no cause for real grief or sadness lies outside of ourselves. What we *are,* no circumstances can take from us.

110. Alcott disliked this Confederate patient. Ibid., 38–39.

ఎ
Union Hospital
January 9, 1863

My Dear Neddie,

I have been sick, or you should have heard from me sooner. Only think how near you are to me. Why don't you get a furlough for a few days and come see me? I think you better write to Miss Stevenson. I don't agree with Alice about the state pay, and I wish if it can be, to be secured to me, or you, [or] Alice, as you please. I am doing my last work now. The tax upon us women who work for the love of it is tremendous when we have a new arrival of wounded, as on the 17th ult. Miss Kendall has had to go to bed, one knee refusing to walk or bend. . . .

Miss Alcott and I worked together over four dying men and saved all but one, the finest of the four, but whether [due to] our sympathy for the poor fellows, or we took cold, I know not, but we both have pneumonia and have suffered terribly. She is a splendid young woman. Can I send you a bundle? Miss Stevenson gave me a beautiful shirt for you. I should like to send you a pound of tea or some of Kate Whitner's gingerbread if I knew you would get it—can't you come over? . . .

Your loving marm,
H.A.R.

ఎ
January 11, 1863

Dear Alice,

Have not had time to write before, the house has been very sick and we nurses have fairly run down. Miss Kendall is in her room, to rest for a day or two. She would not give up till her knee fairly refused to bend at all! And so she is in bed, much to my relief. Miss Alcott, of Concord, began to cough as soon as she got here. The whole house of patients, some in with lung irritations, [were similarly afflicted] and with her at first I thought it was purely sympathetic. Today she has "orders" from me not to leave her room and has a mustard plaster all over her chest. As for myself, the "head surgeon" placed me "under arrest" the day before New Years and visits me twice a day. Mrs. Boyce wanted me to go home with her, but he would not yield. I have a promise that by next Sabbath I may go. My last patient, who was so crazy, whose hand I held so long till he fell asleep, upset me. It was, the Doctor said, "the drop too much." But the boy is doing well, and came and took tea by my bed last night. My experience of sickness has been (not romantic) what so many cows have died of within the last year—pneumonia. I am glad the poor things died, but very glad I did not, for your sake, my precious little girl.

I have had the devoted attention of the whole house, and all the surgeons say even if I can't do anything at all, I *must stay* or the house will go down![111] Stuff. I think the rest will do me good. Mercy! What do the women at home know of work? *We never* stopped till the whole house were pronounced doing well.[112] Now we can afford to lie by for a week. There is no patient who don't know [that] at any hour of night or day they could send to me—that makes them feel comfortable and so they recuperate. . . . Our weather is soft as June, and clear sunshine; still, not as healthy as the summer. I don't like the condition of anything and shall go home as soon as your *warm* time comes.

Your mother

• But Hannah Ropes never did go home. Instead, she had been correct when writing that she had done her "last work." Her illness, however, was not intitially viewed as especially serious. Alice Ropes was summoned to help care for her mother, but when writing to Edward on January 19, 1863, she gave no indication of fear for her recovery:

111. Alcott, too, mentioned that she was well treated by the surgeons during her illness. Ibid., 100.

112. Nurses did a great deal of demanding work and often developed a mild contempt for the women at home. See, for example, Hancock, *South After Gettysburg,* 15, 25, and Wormeley, *The Other Side of the War,* 80, 119.

. . . Mother has been ill for some weeks and indeed nearly all the nurses are ill, so they sent for me to help a little. Miss Dix does not allow young people in the hospital unless very ugly; but she lets me stay during the daytime, which is not very complimentary to my good looks, and I stay at Mrs. Boyce's, quite near the hospital, nights.

If you can obtain a furlough I hope you will come up to see us; it would be a great pleasure to mother and, of course, to me, too, so be sure and come if you can; the hospital is the "Union," at the corner of Bridge and Washington Streets. The horsecars go directly by the door.

• Ropes's condition was also of only mild concern to her friends in Massachusetts. The same day that Alice penned the above letter to Edward, George Sumner wrote to her mother:

My Dear Mrs. Ropes,

I was greatly pained to hear how ill you had been, and was thinking seriously of going on to nurse you, when fortunately Miss Alice forestalled me, and is now, I am sure, administering to you all kinds of good moral medicine. I trust you are so well now as to look back upon your illness as a thing entirely of the past. That bitter Saturday which you went through was intended to elevate your self-esteem, by showing you what perils and suffering you had rescued so many others from. You, in your modesty, did not know how much good you were doing, and now through pain you have come to knowledge.

Now the great thing you have to learn is *to spare yourself.* You have been working much too hard, and now *must take rest.* . . .

I am very glad you met Mrs. Boyce, and hope that Miss Alice has already passed many pleasant hours with her and with the gentle Bessie. They are both so kind and good that it quite cheers one up to see them.

The world in Hancock Street goes on pretty much as when you left. My Mother goes out nearly every day and seems about as strong as ten years ago. She will nurse you on your return. . . .[113]

• Sumner, like Alice, seemed unaware that this might be Ropes's final illness. Edward, however, received a telegram on January 20 to come to his mother's bedside. Sent by Senator Henry Wilson's

113. George Sumner to HAR, Jan. 19, 1863, SRC-UCR.

private secretary, and addressed to the commanding officer of the Second Massachusetts Regiment, it said simply that, "Mrs. Ropes Matron of Union Hotel Hospital Georgetown is dying please have her son Edward E Ropes of Co D come immediately."[114] Edward obtained a pass from his company commander on January 25 for a furlough to date from January 28 to January 31. His efforts, however, were too slow to enable him to see his mother. For, on the evening of Tuesday, January 20, 1863, she died.

Henry Wilson's concern for Hannah Ropes was matched by that of his Senate colleague, Charles Sumner. Both statesmen, known among their peers as determined and perhaps cold politicians, showed a warm, personal aspect where the Massachusetts matron was involved. Sumner had great respect for Ropes, and this was reflected in the letter he wrote to her brother the day following her death:

> My dear Chandler,
> On leaving the Senate yesterday, I went at once to Georgetown, as I mentioned in my telegram. I found Mrs. Ropes very feeble & speaking with difficulty. I could not understand all that she said. I told her of my effort to obtain a furlough for Edward, but that his regiment was in motion, so that he could not now be reached. After I had left her room, & while I was still in the outer room, she expressed a desire to see me again. I hastened to her bedside, when she said clearly, "If you hear anything about Edward let me know." It seemed to me as if she thought from what I said that Edward was in battle.
> Her disease was pneumonia & her lungs were much oppressed. She asked the Doctor while I was there if he could not give her relief. He told me as I was leaving, about half past 5 o'clock, that she could not live through the night. About 9 o'clock in the evening Wilson went out to her & found she had just died. I had already given instructions with regard to her remains.
> The funeral services were this morning. Both Wilson & myself were occupied with public duties, but Major Poor, the clerk of my Committee, attended at my request. Mrs. Ropes had been anxious to provide proper company for Alice on her return. Had any person accidentally here from Boston been on the point of returning I should have taken advantage

---

114. Zenas W. Bliss to Commanding Officer, 2d Mass., Gordon's Brigade, Jan. 20, 1863, SRC-UCR.

of this opportunity. But on inquiry I found no such person, & I at once took advantage of the offer from our private secretary, A.B. Johnson, who leaves his own wife & children & duties here to accompany her. It is now nearly 3 o'clock, & I presume that they are already in the train which starts at this hour.

Mrs. Ropes was a remarkable character, noble & beautiful, & I doubt if she has ever appeared more so than while she has been here in Washington, nursing soldiers. I regret much that incessant & most onerous duties here prevented me from seeing as much of her as I desired. God bless you![115]

• Ropes's illness caused much anxiety among her friends inside and outside of Union Hospital. A detailed account of her final day of life was written to Charles Sumner's mother by Mrs. M.M. Boyce, the friend whom Ropes had so often mentioned in her diary and letters.[116] Writing on January 23, 1863, she related:

My dear Mrs. Sumner,

. . . Ere this, you have doubtless learned the fatal termination of Mrs. Ropes' illness, owing to the circumstances of her situation, so far from her relatives & early friends. I feel it almost a duty to communicate to you what little I saw of the progress of events after the arrival of Alice. I do not think Mrs. Ropes was considered dangerously ill then. If she was, I was not aware of it; she appeared to me to improve slightly for a few days, but I was not then so much with her. I thought it best to leave the long parted ones alone together & when I was there I found the effort Mrs. Ropes made to talk was painful & injurious.

Last Saturday there was a sudden change of weather. Whether she felt it or not, I cannot tell, but she had a relapse of all the worst feelings—violent pain through the chest & increased difficulty of breathing! Fresh blisters were applied & everything done that could be thought of, but with no good result. She never rallied & on Monday evening all hope was abandoned by the medical men, who pronounced her sinking! I think from that time her intense suffering subsided &

115. Charles Sumner to "My dear Chandler" [either Theophilus Parsons Chandler or Peleg Whitman Chandler], Jan. 21, 1863, SRC-UCR.

116. Alcott recorded merely that "Mrs. R. died, . . ." Alcott, *Louisa May Alcott*, 119.

by slow degrees almost ceased. She could not speak without difficulty, but she breathed more naturally & her countenance lost the impression of pain. I was with her a great part of the last day (Tuesday) & found it hard to believe her case so hopeless; so much strength still remained. She could not only move in bed, but, with assistance, arose twice while I was there & sat up in a large chair, evidently relieved by the change of position. When I left in the afternoon she was still up, having her hair combed, & seemed so tranquil that I went home under the hope of finding her the same, next day. She expired before midnight. I sent the carriage, with our old nurse, at breakfast time next morning for Alice—a fearful storm was prevailing through which she came, merely to gather up her things & go back again to the Hospital, to prepare for departure with the precious burthen at 2 P.M.

Mr. Sumner had made all necessary arrangements. Mr. Channing performed the funeral service in the large hall, where were congregated all the poor patients & nurses who were able to attend.[117] Afterwards, poor Alice had about one hour's rest (in the arms of Miss Kendall, pressed to her bosom like a poor unhappy child) before she left in charge of Mr. & Mrs. Johnston.[118] I am very anxious about Alice! She has shown such extraordinary firmness & composure that the reaction may be serious when it comes & she has had no relief from *trials*! At the time her dear mother breathed her last she had a very violent paroxysm indeed, when an anodyne was given her & she soon fell asleep—she had been up two nights previous. I have been unhappy at not having Mrs. Ropes under my own roof; but this feeling has changed since conversing with the kind surgeon who attended her so faithfully. He said there was a peculiar fitness in her dying at her post of duty, surrounded by the associations endeared to her. Could she have chosen, she probably would have had it so. I feel satisfied, too, that she has had the advantage of good surgeons & nurses alway, on the spot to watch any change. No children could have done more for her than her two attached nurses, Mrs. Hopkins & Mrs. Warren. Everyone about the place

117. This was William Henry Channing, of Boston, a Unitarian minister and nephew of William Ellery Channing. He was chaplain of Stanton Hospital, Washington, D.C., 1862–1865, and served as chaplain for the U.S. House of Representatives from 1863 to 1864.

118. Boyce refers to A.B. Johnson, secretary for Charles Sumner. See Charles Sumner to "My dear Chandler," Jan. 21, 1863, SRC-UCR.

looked up to her with affection & reverence, & her influence over the roughest even, among "her boys," as she loved to call them, was remarkable. Whether the great fatigue & privation of comfort during the last six months of her precious life made her less able to resist such an attack no one would like to decide. I shall always feel that she has given up her life to her country, as freely as anyone who died on the field. "True soldier of the Lord!"[119]

• Boyce's sentiments would undoubtedly have been gratifying to Ropes, but those she might best have appreciated were expressed by her children, Edward and Alice, in late January 1863. If Ropes had held her own mother in particular esteem, so did Edward and Alice suffer greatly upon her departure and remember her in the kindest of terms. Alice was particularly upset that her brother had not been able to visit their mother before her death. She therefore penned the following lines to him—in phrases which reflected her own and Ropes's Swedenborgian faith—describing the matron's last days and attempting to soothe his grief.

Brookline, Massachusetts
January 27, 1863

My Darling Brother,

I love you very much but feel that *that* will be but small comfort to you and will poorly fill the void created by our dear mother's passing from our bodily vision. But, darling, she is with us all the time, and can tell us our duty and see how much we love her without the use of words, which are so apt to hide more than convey our meaning.

We did not feel that she was really dangerously ill until the day before she died. Then Mr. Sumner made every endeavor to reach you, or send a dispatch, but Stanton said the regiment was on the march and he could not tell where you were. I had felt sure that you would receive some message and would come in time. Indeed, [I] did not give up the hope until the very last. My thoughts were with you all the time, for it was so hard for you not to see her. She suffered very much for breath and we were almost relieved when the end came. It was very peaceful and very beautiful. I think she must have

---

119. M.M. Boyce to "My dear Mrs. Sumner," Jan. 23, 1863, SRC-UCR. According to another observer, "She has died for her country, as much as the soldier shot in battle." Theophilus Parsons to Peleg Whitman Chandler, Jan 24, 1863, SRC-UCR.

found so many dear friends all ready and glad to receive her. How happy, how rested she must feel. It seems as though she were saying to me all the time, "Child, I am so happy." The nurses were very devoted. Three of those she loved best gave all their time to her, and they wanted me to tell her friends that no hired hands ever touched her during her sickness, [n]or did anything occur to jar upon her heart in anything. The surgeons were very attentive and Dr. Perley came over from Washington every day. I thought she would stay much longer, she seemed to still have so much strength, and when I wrote to you I thought she would be here several weeks. The others knew more about such things. She talked of you a great deal, longing to see you once more, until the last day—she seemed more in the other world than this and took very little notice of anyone.

Don't think you have nothing to live for now, for you *must* live for me. I need you very much, and hope you will need me. Whenever you want me I am at your disposal. My life now belongs to you and father, if he is living. And we must try to fit ourselves to go to mother in a few years. Perhaps we shall never rise so high as she, but our love for her will take us to her, and her great and now divine love for us will be leading us up until our discipline here below is finished.[120]

• While Alice wrote from Massachusetts, Edward was in Washington, D.C., where he learned of Ropes's death. "God has taken our mother to himself," he told Alice on January 28, "and I am here only too late, too late." He had seen Senators Wilson and Sumner, who offered their condolences. But, he said, "I could not talk. . . . Good Night, Sister. Do not mourn for our mother, for she is happy."[121] This brief missive was followed the next day by another, in which Edward told his sister that "Mother was near me last night. It seemed as if I was a little boy, playing on the floor, and mother was sitting, as if knitting, and looking at me very thoughtfully. It seemed also as if she was needed somewhere else, for she did not stay long. It does seem as if mother was nearer to me now than ever before."[122]

120. Alice Ropes joined the Boston Society of the New Jerusalem on Jan. 6, 1861. See *A Sketch of the History of the Boston Society of the New Jerusalem*, 85.
121. EER to ASR, Jan. 28, 1863, SRC-UCR.
122. EER to ASR, Jan. 29, 1863, SRC-UCR.

Alice responded to her brother's note of the twenty-eighth on January 30. "I am glad you saw Mr. Sumner," she said. "He was so kind, very different from the cold statesman that he appears to the world." Ropes's body, she noted, had been taken to New Glouces-ter and buried "by Grandpa's. It was in the old graveyard made in the year mother was born, just a little way from Grandpa's house. I think she would have liked it so." If Edward ever had occasion to visit Georgetown, she continued, he must "call at the hospital," for "you would hear many pleasant things of mother from the nurses and her *boys*—you would see how they loved her and how kind they were during her illness."[123]

The war, then, was finished for Hannah Ropes. It went on, however, for her children. Edward continued to serve with his regiment, which saw action at such places as Chancellorsville, Gettysburg, Atlanta, and Savannah.[124] Alice, meanwhile, urged by the Sumner family, traveled to New Bern, North Carolina, to teach the newly emancipated blacks. Ropes's children carried on her struggle for national victory, abolition of slavery, and a new defini-tion of American freedom. Had the matron been there to observe them, it seems fair to suggest that she would surely "have liked it so."

123. ASR to EER, Jan. 30, 1863, SRC-UCR.
124. Dyer, *Compendium,* III, 1248–49.

Glossary of
Names Mentioned by
Hannah Ropes

Alice—Alice Shephard Ropes, Hannah Ropes's daughter.

Alley—Congressman John B. Alley, of Massachusetts.

Aunt Eliza—Elizabeth Schlatter Chandler, Hannah Ropes's sister-in-law and wife of Theophilus Parsons Chandler.

Banks—Congressman and General Nathaniel P. Banks, of Massachusetts.

Barnards (Mr. Barnard, Mrs. Barnard)—George M. Barnard, a Boston merchant, and his wife, Susan.

Bessie (Miss Boyce)—Bessie Boyce, daughter of Mrs. M.M. Boyce, of Georgetown, D.C.

Buffington—Congressman James Buffington, of Massachusetts.

Burnside—Major General Ambrose E. Burnside, commander of Union forces at the Battle of Fredericksburg.

Cashman—Sarah J. Cashman, a nurse in Union Hospital.

Charles Sumner (Charles, Sumner)—Senator Charles Sumner, of Massachusetts, chairman of the Senate Foreign Relations Committee during the Civil War.

Charlie—Major Charles Peleg Chandler, First Massachusetts Volunteer Infantry Regiment, Hannah Ropes's nephew.

Charlie Lyon—Captain Charles Lyon Chandler, Thirty-fourth Massachusetts Volunteer Infantry Regiment, Hannah Ropes's nephew.

Chase—Salmon P. Chase, secretary of the United States Treasury.

Daremus—Julia Daremus, a nurse in Union Hospital.

Derby—Captain Richard Derby, Fifteenth Massachusetts Volunteer Infantry Regiment.

Dick Chute—Lieutenant Richard Henry Chute, Fifty-ninth Massachusetts Volunteer Infantry Regiment, Hannah Ropes's nephew.

Dixon—Senator James F. Dixon, of Connecticut.

Dr. Clark (Head Surgeon, Superior Surgeon)—A.M. Clark, assistant surgeon, United States Volunteers, and head surgeon, Union Hospital, September 16–November 8, 1862.

Dr. Hays—William Hays, acting assistant surgeon, who

served in Union Hospital from June 17 to August 17, 1862.

Dr. Hinkle—A.G.B. Hinkle, volunteer surgeon from Philadelphia, who assisted in Union Hospital for a short period in the Fall of 1862.

Dr. Kennedy—James F. Kennedy, assistant surgeon, United States Army, in charge of Union Hospital from July 16 to September 16, 1862.

Dr. Ottman—R. Ottman, acting assistant surgeon, who served in Union Hospital from September 12, 1862 to February 19, 1863, and was in charge of the hospital from Saturday to Monday, November 8– 10, 1862.

Dr. Stipp—George W. Stipp, surgeon, United States Volunteers; head surgeon of Union Hospital, following departure of A.M. Clark, November 10, 1862– March 27, 1863.

Fannie—(Fannie Candler)—Frances Vaughan Chandler, Hannah Ropes's niece, married in August 1862 to William L. Candler and thereafter referred to as Fannie Candler.

Fanny—Mrs. P.H. Warren, a nurse in Union Hospital (s.v. Mrs. Warren).

Frémont—Major General John C. Frémont.

George—George Sumner, brother of Massachusetts Senator Charles Sumner.

Governor Andrew—John A. Andrew, governor of Massachusetts.

Grandma (Mother)—Esther Parsons Chandler, Hannah Ropes's mother.

Hale—Senator John P. Hale, of New Hampshire.

J. Thomas Stevenson—prominent Boston merchant whose sister, Hannah E. Stevenson, served with Hannah Ropes in Union Hospital.

Julia Sumner—sister of Massachusetts Senator Charles Sumner.

Louis—Louis Herman, attached as cook to Union Hospital on August 8, 1862.

McClellan—Major General George B. McClellan.

Medical Inspector (Inspector, Dr. Perley)—Thomas F. Perley, medical inspector general, United States Army, April 1862– August 1863.

Miss Alcott—Louisa May Alcott, of Massachusetts, a nurse in Union Hospital, author of *Hospital Sketches* (Boston, 1863) and subsequent popular works.

Miss Best—Margaret Best, a nurse in Union Hospital.

Miss Boyce—Bessie Boyce (s.v. Bessie).

Miss Dix—Dorothea Dix.

Miss Kendall—Julia C. Kendall, of Plymouth, Massachusetts, a nurse in Union Hospital.

Miss Low—apparently a transient nurse staying temporarily with Hannah Ropes in Union Hospital.

Miss Stevenson—Hannah E. Stevenson, of Boston, a nurse in Union Hospital.

Mr. Barrett—Private Richard Barrett, Fifteenth Massachusetts Volunteer Infantry Regiment, a patient in Union Hospital.

Mr. Channing—William Henry Channing, Unitarian minister and chaplain of Stanton Hospital, Washington, D.C., 1862– 1865.

Mr. Hooper—Congressman Samuel Hooper, of Massachusetts.

Mrs. Boyce—M.M. Boyce, a widow and owner of the "Montrose" estate on Georgetown Heights.

Mrs. Hopkins—Edith A. Hopkins, a nurse in Union Hospital and apparently the "pretty widow" to whom Ropes occasionally refers.

Mrs. Sumner—Relief Jacob (Mrs. Charles Pinckney) Sumner, mother of Massachusetts Senator Charles Sumner.

Mrs. Warren—Mrs. P.H. Warren, a nurse in Union Hospital, to whom Hannah Ropes also refers as "Fanny," or the "needle woman."

Ned (Neddie)—Edward Elson Ropes, Hannah Ropes's son.

Peleg—Peleg Whitman Chandler, of Boston, Hannah Ropes's younger brother.

Pope—Major General John Pope, commander of the Army of Virginia during the Second Battle of Bull Run (Second Manassas).

Porter—Major General Fitz-John Porter.

Powers—Private Joshua Powers, F Company, Tenth New Hampshire Volunteer Infantry Regiment, a patient in Union Hospital.

Rice—Congressman Alexander H. Rice, of Massachusetts.

Sigel—Major General Franz Sigel.

Stanton (Secretary Stanton)—Edwin M. Stanton, United States secretary of war.

Surgeon General—Brigadier General William A. Hammond, surgeon general, United States Army, 1862–1864.

Thoph—Theophilus Parsons Chandler, of Boston, Hannah Ropes's older brother.

Train—Congressman Charles R. Train, of Massachusetts.

Trevor—Corporal Richard Trevor, F Company, Thirty-first New York Volunteers, attached to Union Hospital on July 5, 1862 and assigned position of Wardmaster.

Wade—Senator Benjamin F. Wade, of Ohio.

Wilson (General Wilson)—Senator Henry Wilson, of Massachusetts, chairman of the Senate Committee on Military Affairs during the Civil War.

Abbreviations

For convenient reference, the following acronymns are used to designate particular persons, collections, and source repositories:

ASR   Alice S. Ropes
EPC   Esther Parsons Chandler
EER   Edward E. Ropes
FRC   Federal Records Center, Laguna Niguel, California
HAR   Hannah A. Ropes
IMO-NA   Index of Medical Officers, Contract Physicians, and Hospital Stewards (Union Hospital), Record Group 112 (Records of the Surgeon General's Office, Medical Inspector's Office), National Archives, Washington, D.C.
MR-NA   Muster Rolls for Union Hospital, Letters Sent and Received by the Surgeon, Registers of Patients, Record Group 94 (Records of the Adjutant General's Office, 1780s–1917), National Archives, Washington, D.C.
SRC-UCR   Skinner-Ropes Manuscript Collection, Special Collections Division, General Library, University of California, Riverside.

Bibliography

The Skinner-Ropes Manuscript Collection, located in the Special Collections Department of the General Library, University of California, Riverside, was the principal source for this volume. Also useful, in determining details concerning particular individuals mentioned by Ropes, were the records of the Federal Census for 1860, available on microfilm at the Federal Records Center, Laguna Niguel, California. The National Archives, Washington, D.C., contains sources pertinent to a study of the Union Hospital and wartime medical service in general. Those specifically useful for this work were "Compiled Military Service Records, Hospital Attendants, Matrons and Nurses (Civil War)" and "Muster Rolls for Union Hospital, Letters Sent and Received by the Surgeon, Registers of Patients," in Record Group 94 (Records of the Adjutant General's Office, 1780s–1917), and "Index of Medical Officers, Contract Physicians, and Hospital Stewards (Union Hospital)," in Record Group 112 (Records of the Surgeon General's Office, Medical Inspector's Office).

Hannah Ropes's two publications—*Six Months in Kansas: By a Lady* (Boston: John P. Jewett, 1856), and *Cranston House: A Novel* (Boston: Otis Clapp, 1859)—were fundamental to incisive perspective upon the matron, while Louisa May Alcott's *Hospital Sketches* (Boston: James Redpath, 1863) reveals further information concerning Union Hospital and Ropes's nursing activities. An invaluable resource regarding the Civil War medical situation is *The Medical and Surgical History of the War of the Rebellion, 1861–65*, issued by the United States Surgeon General's Office, 2 vols. in 6 pts. (Washington, D.C.: Government Printing Office, 1870–83). Other works used in composing this study are listed below.

Adams, George Worthington. *Doctors in Blue: The Medical History of the Union Army in the Civil War*. New York: Henry Schuman, 1952.

Alcott, Louisa May. *Louisa May Alcott: Her Life, Letters and Journals*. Ed. Ednah D. Cheney. Boston: Little, Brown, 1928.

Anthony, Katharine. *Louisa May Alcott*. New York: Knopf, 1938.

Benjamin, Marcus, ed. *Washington During War Time: A Series of Papers Showing the Military, Political and Social Phases During 1861 to 1865*. Washington, D.C.: National Tribune, [1902].

Bolton, Sarah K. *Lives of Girls Who Became Famous*. New York: Crowell, 1886.

Boyd, Andrew. *Boyd's Washington and Georgetown Directory, 1864*. Washington, D.C.: Hudson Taylor, 1863.

Brooks, Noah. *Mr. Lincoln's Washington: Selections from the Writings of Noah Brooks, Civil War Correspondent*. Ed. P.J. Staudenraus. New York: Yoseloff, 1967.

———. *Washington, D.C., in Lincoln's Time*. Ed. Herbert Mitgang. Chicago: Quadrangle Books, 1971.

Commager, Henry Steele, introd. *The Official Atlas of the Civil War*. New York: Yoseloff, 1958.

Congressional Globe, 2d Sess., 37th Congress, 1862. Washington, D.C.: John C. Rives, 1862.

Dyer, Frederick H. *A Compendium of the War of the Rebellion*. 3 vols. 1908; rpt. New York: n.p., 1959.

Eisenschiml, Otto. *The Celebrated Case of Fitz-John Porter: An American Dreyfus Affair*. Indianapolis: Bobbs-Merrill, 1950.

Emerson, Joseph. *Female Education: A Discourse Delivered at the Dedication of the Seminary Hall in Saugus, Jan. 15, 1822.* Boston: Samuel T. Armstrong, and Crocker & Brewster, 1823.

Goodsell, Willystine, ed. *Pioneers of Women's Education in the United States: Emma Willard, Catherine Beecher, Mary Lyon.* 1931; rpt. New York: AMS Press, 1970.

Greenbie, Marjorie Barstow. *Lincoln's Daughters of Mercy.* New York: Putnam's, 1944.

Hancock, Cornelia. *South After Gettysburg: Letters of Cornelia Hancock from the Army of the Potomac.* Ed. Henrietta S. Jaquette. Philadelphia: n.p., 1937.

Hutchinson's Washington and Georgetown Directory, 1863. Washington, D.C.: Hutchinson & Bro., 1863.

Kimmel, Stanley. *Mr. Lincoln's Washington.* New York: Coward-McCann, 1957.

Leech, Margaret. *Reveille in Washington, 1860–1865.* Rpt. New York: Grosset & Dunlap, 1941.

Lincoln, Abraham. *The Collected Works of Abraham Lincoln.* Ed. Roy P. Basler et al. 8 vols. New Brunswick, N.J.: Rutgers Univ. Press, 1953.

Livermore, Mary A. *My Story of the War.* Hartford, Conn.: A.D. Worthington, 1890.

Long, E.B., with Barbara Long. *The Civil War Day by Day: An Almanac, 1861–1865.* Garden City, N.Y: Doubleday, 1971.

Lowell, Mary Chandler. *Chandler-Parsons: Edmond Chaundeler, Geoffrey Parsons and Allied Families.* Boston: T.R. Marvin & Son, 1911.

McClellan, George B. *McClellan's Own Story.* New York: Charles L. Webster, 1887.

Massachusetts Adjutant General Office. *Record of the Massachusetts Volunteers, 1861–1865.* 2 vols. Boston: Wright & Potter, 1868–70.

Maxwell, William Quentin. *Lincoln's Fifth Wheel: The Political History of the U.S. Sanitary Commission.* New York: Longmans, Green, 1956.

Moore, Frank. *Women of the War: Their Heroism and Self-Sacrifice.* Hartford, Conn.: S.S. Scranton, 1866.

Nightingale, Florence. *Notes on Nursing: What It Is, and What It Is Not.* New York: D. Appleton, 1860.

Pierce, Edward L. *Memoir and Letters of Charles Sumner.* 4 vols. Boston: Roberts Brothers, 1877–93.

Riddle, Albert Gallatin. *Recollections of War Times: Reminiscences of Men and Events in Washington, 1860–1865.* New York: Putnam's, 1895.

Shannon, Fred Albert. *The Organization and Administration of the Union Army, 1861–1865.* 2 vols. 1928; rpt. Gloucester, Mass.: Peter Smith, 1965.

A Sketch of the History of the Boston Society of the New Jerusalem with A List of its Members. Boston: John C. Regan, 1873.

Smith, Adelaide W. *Reminiscences of An Army Nurse During the Civil War.* New York: Graves Publishing Co., 1911.

Steiner, Paul E. *Physician-Generals in the Civil War: A Study in Nineteenth Mid-Century American Medicine.* Springfield, Ill.: Charles C. Thomas, 1966.

Stern, Madeleine B. *Louisa May Alcott.* Norman: Univ. of Oklahoma Press, 1950.

Stern, Philip Van Doren. *Soldier Life in the Union and Confederate Armies.* Bloomington: Indiana Univ. Press, 1961.

Stewart, Isabel M., and Anne L. Austin. *A History of Nursing from Ancient to Modern Times: A World View.* 5th ed. New York: Putnam's, 1962.

Stillé, Charles J. *History of the United States Sanitary Commission: Being the General Report of its Work During the War of the Rebellion.* Philadelphia: Lippincott, 1866.

Thompson, William Y. "The U.S. Sanitary Commission." *Civil War History* 2, No. 2 (June 1956), 41–64.

U.S. Adjutant General Office. *Official Army Register of the Volunteer Force of the United States Army for the Years 1861, '62, '63, '64, '65.* 8 vols. Washington, D.C.: Adjutant General Office, 1865–67.

U.S. Sanitary Commission. *Documents of the U.S. Sanitary*

Commission. 3 vols. New York and Cleveland: n.p., 1866–71.

———. *The Sanitary Commission of the United States Army: A Succinct Narrative of its Work and Purposes.* 1864; rpt. New York: Arno Press-New York Times, 1972.

The War of the Rebellion: A Compilation of the Official Records of the Union and Confederate Armies. 70 vols. in 128 books. Washington, D.C.: Government Printing Office, 1880–1901.

Ware, Edith Ellen. *Political Opinion in Massachusetts During Civil War and Reconstruction.* 1916; rpt. New York: AMS Press, 1968.

Warner, Ezra J. *Generals in Blue: Lives of the Union Commanders.* Baton Rouge: Louisiana State Univ. Press, 1964.

Washington, D.C.: A Guide to the Nation's Capital. American Guide Series. New York: Hastings House, 1942.

Watson, William. *Letters of a Civil War Surgeon.* Ed. Paul Fatout. Lafayette, Ind.: Purdue Research Foundation, 1961.

Wells, Damon. *Stephen Douglas: The Last Years, 1857–1861.* Austin: Univ. of Texas Press, 1971.

Whetten, Harriet Douglas. "A Volunteer Nurse in the Civil War: The Diary of Harriet Douglas Whetten." Ed. Paul H. Hass. *Wisconsin Magazine of History* 48 (1965), 205–21.

———. "A Volunteer Nurse in the Civil War: The Letters of Harriet Douglas Whetten." Ed. Paul H. Hass. *Wisconsin Magazine of History* 48 (1964), 131–51.

Whitman, Walt. *Walt Whitman's Memoranda During the War [&] Death of Abraham Lincoln.* Ed. Roy P. Basler. Bloomington: Indiana Univ. Press, 1962.

———. *The Wound Dresser.* Ed. Richard M. Bucke. 1897; rpt. New York: Bodley Press, 1949.

Wiley, Bell Irvin. *The Life of Billy Yank: The Common Soldier of the Union.* Indianapolis: Bobbs-Merrill, 1952.

Wood, Ann Douglas. "The War Within a War: Women Nurses in the Union Army." *Civil War History* 18, No. 3 (Sept. 1972), 197–212.

Woody, Thomas. *A History of Women's Education in the United States.* 2 vols. 1929; rpt. New York: Octagon Books, 1966.
Woolsey, Jane Stuart. *Hospital Days.* New York: Van Nostrand, 1870.
Wormeley, Katharine Prescott. *The Other Side of the War with the Army of the Potomac.* Boston: Ticknor, 1889.
Worthington, Marjorie. *Miss Alcott of Concord: A Biography.* Garden City, N.Y.: Doubleday, 1958.

Index

Civil War Nurse was typeset on the Variable Input Photo-typesetter in eleven-point Garamond No.3 with one-point line spacing. Bookman Italic was used for display. The book was designed by Jim Billingsley, composed by Williams, Chattanooga, Tennessee, printed offset by Thomson-Shore, Inc., Dexter, Michigan, and bound by John H. Dekker & Sons, Grand Rapids, Michigan. The paper on which the book is printed bears the watermark of S. D. Warren.

THE UNIVERSITY OF TENNESSEE PRESS

KNOXVILLE